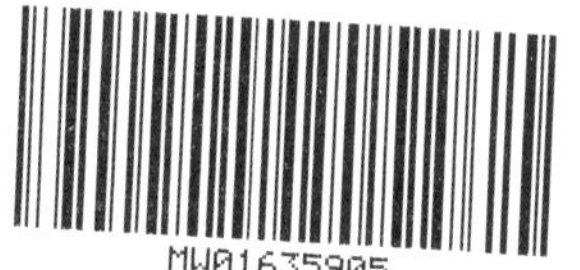

RUIN YOUR LIFE

by Jack Cameron

06/04/14

RUIN YOUR LIFE

Cover and book design by Jack Cameron

Edited by Bridget Howe

Published by

Table 30 Productions in association with
Dark Repast Publications

www.jackcameron.com

Printed
by CreateSpace.com in U.S.A.

Cameron, Jack

Ruin Your Life / Jack Cameron -3rd ed.
ISBN-13: 978-1-49-610542-4

May you live in interesting times.
-Ancient Chinese Curse

Disclaimer

Following the advice of my lawyer, I begin this book by saying that I do not suggest you do any of the things mentioned in this book, or that if you do, you at the very least understand that I have told you not to do them. More to the point, if you should find yourself about to be apprehended by those fine men and women in law enforcement, please burn this book and forget about its existence. This book is about Ruining Your Life, not mine. I can ruin my own life all by myself. So if you happen to take the advice in this book and discover that your life has been ruined, well don't blame me.

I'd also like to point out that as much as possible, I tried to make this book for both men and women. When I absolutely had to refer to a gender, I chose to write like a white heterosexual male because coincidentally I am a white heterosexual male. But once again, regardless of what gender, race, religion, or height you are, if you do the things I mention in this book, you're on your own. I can't be responsible for your actions. If I were, believe me you'd be doing more for me than reading my book. And what a wonderful world it would be.

Unfortunately, you all have free will. But given that you have read this far in the disclaimer, I'll give you the very first way to ruin your life: Take the blame. Don't try to blame the music you listen to, the video games you play, the movies you watch, or the books you read. Take responsibility for your actions and laugh when they ask if you feel bad about what you did. Like my first girlfriend said: "It's all your fault."

-Jack Cameron

Table of Contents

Part 1

Into The Abyss

Go to any bookstore and you will find entire sections devoted to self-help books. After reading these books, you will have the tools to make your life better. No matter what problem you might have you can bet someone has written a book about how to therapeutically resolve the matter and live a healthier, happier life.

But let's face it; most of us don't really believe a book is going to help us. Most of us don't want someone trying to tell us how to face our inner demons and nurture our inner child. And those who do need to grow up and try living once in a while. What is needed is not a voice to tell you how to live a healthy, happy life, but how to live an interesting life. When you go to the movies or watch your favorite TV show, do the characters have perfect well-adjusted lives? Of course not. Perfect lives are not interesting lives. You want to know why people who have 'everything going for them' kill themselves? Because they are bored. They have achieved what they've been told to achieve. They have the good grades, good job, nice car, 2.5 kids, and the house in the suburbs. And they are bored off their ass. They've been to the mountaintop and found that it's just really cold and lonely.

I for one do not want to live a healthy, happy life. I want things to be fairly screwed up. I want to have problems. I want to get myself in huge messes and then marvel at how I get out of them or how I live with them. I like making mistakes and doing things the wrong way if only to find out what will happen. One of my best friends in the world never agrees with my decisions and hates everything I do. But she also wants to hear about the latest thing that's happened to me if only to live vicariously through my exploits.

My name is Jack Cameron. I'm a guy who got married at the age of twenty, divorced at twenty-one, and went on a bender that left my aunt's house half-destroyed, a car on fire, and a high school girls swim team drunk and incoherent. I've been in twenty-six car accidents. I've been shot at on three separate occasions. I've woken up in an alley wrapped in a beer banner in Seattle on New Year's Day.

I've willingly walked through a two mile train tunnel knowing full well that a train was coming. I've woken up on an airplane over the Pacific Ocean with no idea how I got there. I have dined with millionaires with only two dollars in my pocket and made a thousand dollar decision with the flip of a coin. In other words, I am damn good at ruining my life and if you listen carefully to what I tell you, you can ruin yours too and have the best time you've ever had doing it. This is not self-help. This is self-destruct. In time, you'll thank me.

Chapter 1

Bring Tools

Ruining your life is like robbing a bank: you can do it with nothing, but it's a lot easier if you bring a few tools. Over the years I've learned that there are certain items in this world that are worth more than their weight in gold. These things can get you out of unpleasant situations and, quite honestly into some genuinely fucked up situations. On the other hand, there are times they may save your life, which is a good thing since it's fairly difficult to ruin your life if it's over.

DO NOT BRING:

Before we start talking about things you should have, I think it's important to go over a few things you should not have.

A Gun

There are those who say that a gun is the great equalizer and that it is better to have a gun and not need it than need a gun and not have it. There is a certain truth to that. But the fact remains that having a gun will make you more likely to get into a situation where you need (or at least think you need) a gun. Those situations tend to end with somebody dead. And the guy left behind has prison or a large lawyer's bill to look forward to.

We're here to make your life more interesting, not to make you a murderer because believe it or not, murderers are not interesting. They're just desperate and stupid and let's just assume that you aren't.

A Motorcycle

I realize that motorcycles are definitely cool, but my mom used to be a trauma nurse in the E.R. and she used to tell me how the doctors called motorcycles 'donor-cycles'. Helmet or no helmet, there aren't a lot of bikers out there that have had two bad motorcycle wrecks. And I'm trying to ruin your life not get you killed.

Having a cool vehicle is definitely part of ruining your life and we'll get to that in a moment but for now, understand that motorcycles are not a good idea in today's 'soccer-mom-on-a-cellphone-driving-big-SUV-world'.

Hardcore Drugs

Cocaine, heroin, and meth may seem like good ways to ruin your life but it's a one hit wonder. You don't want to be a junkie. Junkies are boring. Junkies are just going from fix to fix and nothing else in the world matters. Not money, not friends, not even sex. That's just stupid. Especially when there are plenty of other drugs that cost less money and don't turn you into a drug addict.

It's not that drugs are bad for you. This is the 21st century. Everything is bad for you. It isn't like you're going to live forever anyway. But getting hooked on hardcore drugs is like getting hooked on masturbation. After a while it's not as much fun and no one wants to be around you.

DO BRING:

So below are a few things that not only make ruining your life a lot easier, they make it more fun. None of them are too terribly expensive or rare. They're things you want to have in case of emergency or boredom.

Zippo Lighter

This one is simple. Making fire is what made us better than the other monkeys in caveman days. The distinctive sound of a Zippo lighter is unmistakably cool and as long as you're lighting something you might as well look cool doing it. Cigarettes, campfires, and houses all burn better with a Zippo. Trust me.

Also, as a side note, Zippo lighters happen to be guaranteed for life so if you ever happen to break one, you can get it repaired simply by mailing the lighter back to Zippo.

Trench Coat

In ninth grade I bought my first trench coat. I bought it essentially because it was my first year in high school and one of the pastimes of upperclassmen was to toss freshmen into Commencement Bay, which is more than a little cold and polluted. I figured a trench coat might make me look taller and not so much like a freshman. It worked. And as years went by and I bought other coats, I learned that a trench coat could do more than keep me dry in the rain.

There's the storage factor. Carrying a bag or a backpack around gets annoying. Having the right coat with the right amount of pockets makes life a lot easier. Once using a multi-pocketed leather trench coat I put an entire six-pack of beer in my pockets (and the coat already looked so bulky the cashier didn't even notice).

People fear people in trench coats. Cops and hit men wear them in movies. The coat that can carry a bunch of beer can also carry a shotgun. In other words, people don't usually fuck with a guy in a trench coat.

Best of all, a trench coat is a wearable blanket. Walk with your girl to some secluded part of a park or a beach and you have something to put on the ground should you have a thing for public fornication. And it doesn't even look like you planned it.

Also for the comic book geek in us all, trench coats are as close as you can get to wearing a cape without people laughing at you. Though I don't suggest purchasing a bright red trench coat.

A Leather Jacket

You can't wear a trench coat everywhere. If you do, people will start to think you're a bit strange and if you walk by a school once too often, you'll be arrested for 'planning a Columbine' which if you haven't noticed seems to get you in just as much trouble as actually doing it. So it's good to have another coat. That coat should be a leather jacket.

Leather jackets have been cool forever and always will be. They do everything a jacket should do: keep you warm, have lots of storage space, and they're tough enough to protect you from falling off that motorcycle I told you not to get.

You should buy one at a leather shop. This coat should be all leather. No spikes. No tassels. The jacket should be big, functional, and heavy.

A Bottle Opener

If you follow half of the stuff in this book, you'll end up drinking a hell of a lot of beer and not every brewery is nice enough to have twist off lids. Like the Boy Scouts say, be prepared. This one is really a no-brainer, but I figure it's best to still mention it just in case.

A Hundred-Dollar Bill

One of my well-traveled friends told me of this idea. This hundred-dollar bill is not for spending. It is to be kept on your person like a fire alarm. The sign reads: "Break in case of adversity." No matter where you are in the world, a hundred-dollar bill will likely get you a ride out of trouble.

Also, there are times when you've spent your money and the night isn't over. Rather than going home or having to find an ATM somewhere, you know you've got that hundred bucks for dinner, drinks, or a not-quite-high-class prostitute.

A Car Made Before 1979

Recent studies show that teen sexual activity is down in the last few years. The reason for this if you ask me is new cars. Newer cars are built like space capsules. The seats and interior of a new car more resemble the cockpit of a jet than anything else. Only a particularly agile midget could comfortably have sex in a new car.

I've been in car accidents in everything from a Dodge Dart to a new Mustang Convertible. I understand what happens to a vehicle when it collides with another vehicle, when it slides off the road, when it tumbles down a hill into a swamp and sinks, and yes, even when it goes off a cliff and catches fire. All of these scenarios are better if the vehicle you are in is very large and made out of steel. Newer cars have airbags and crumple zones and all sorts of other things that may keep you safe but also destroy your car.

Movie director John Landis said of the two Blues Brothers movies that apart from the first one being a hell of a lot better, the biggest difference between the two movies is that half the cars they crashed in the 1979 Blues Brothers movie could be driven away, whereas in Blues Brothers 2000, every crashed car was totaled. Fuck airbags. Place your faith in American steel. If you drive a '78 Monte Carlo into some new car, I'm betting you won't be the injured one.

Condoms

Like death, sex can come at any time and it's best to be ready. I'm not the biggest fan of condoms but I'm even less of a fan of accidental pregnancies and diseases. To paraphrase gun nuts: it's better to have a condom and not need it than need a condom and not have it.

A Lawyer

If you do even half of the things in this book, you might end up in some legal trouble. What you need isn't necessarily a lawyer who you have to pay a lot of money to. Instead what you want to find is a lawyer who knows the right people for the right situation and can point you in the right direction whenever you need it.

Despite all the jokes about lawyers, it's important to note that not having one can be dangerous and having a bad one is even worse. Ask around. Find a guy who isn't only good in the courtroom but also on the golf course. You want a man (or woman) who knows people.

Something to keep in mind is that unlike cops or spouses you do not ever want to lie to a lawyer. This guy doesn't want to put you in prison. He wants to help keep you out of prison. The more they know, the more they can help. Do whatever your lawyer tells you to do and don't worry about how much money they charge. Debt is better than prison. Always.

There are other tools that I haven't mentioned. Some are mentioned later in the book and others you'll just have to discover for yourself. Now that you're prepared, turn the page and get started. Today is the first day of your own downward spiral. Enjoy it.

Chapter 2

Be A Proper Drunk

If you want to write about ruining your life, you have to talk about alcohol. Alcohol has ruined countless lives. Regardless of where you live or who you are, odds are you know someone who has ruined their life with that most fun of diseases, alcoholism. It is the Great Vice. However, I am not trying to kill my readers so let me tell you how to be a Proper Drunk. This is important. If you're going to do something wrong, do it right.

You don't want to go all out here. Some people think that drinking a bottle of Bacardi 151, stealing a car, and driving it off an overpass at 120mph is a good way to ruin your life. They are wrong. That is a good way to end your life. Drinking and driving under any circumstances is stupid for a lot of reasons, but the biggest and most important to any drunk worth the name is that if you get in a wreck and die, you won't be able to drink tomorrow. If you want to kill yourself, that's your own thing, but don't look for help here. If on the other hand, you're just looking to develop a not so healthy drinking problem, then read on.

Beer

Just because you're a drunk does not mean you have no taste. At no time should you be buying Budweiser or Schlitz or Miller High Life. It doesn't matter how inexpensive it is, it's how cheap it is. As a Proper Drunk, you should be buying beer in the middle of the beer isle. You do not want to buy top quality stuff like Chimay. Not on any sort of regular basis. Beer like that is for special occasions or perhaps to start you off.

You want a good microbrew like Pyramid or Rolling Rock or Red Hook. Try to avoid beers you've seen too many commercials for. (Note: If you throw a party, be sure to make it clear that cheap beer is unacceptable. None of that bringing shitty beer and drinking the good beer stuff. For more on parties see Chapter 13.)

Beer is something that everyone has a different taste in. Figure out what yours is. Do you like dark beer or light beer? Do you like seasonal beer or are you someone who drinks the same kind of beer year round? Most bars have a sampler and any bartender worth his salt should be able to help you find the right beer for you.

Personally, my favorite beer is Rogue's Brutal Bitter, but that's not the kind of beer I can recommend to everyone. Thanks to microbrews there are literally hundreds of beers out there worth trying. Somewhere is the perfect beer for you but given all those choices you should start drinking soon.

Wine

We're talking about being a Proper Drunk. Only suicidal people, teenagers, and rich people who think they are too good for beer get drunk on wine. Still, there are those who are wine drunks so here are a few pointers. White wine isn't really wine. People who like white wine tend to be the same people who like wine coolers. If you must drink wine, make it a red. A good Malbec or something. Remember even number years are better than odd. Not that it really matters for our purposes. We're not talking about savoring here.

If you're getting drunk on wine, you don't want it to be really good wine because really good wine is really expensive. Find something that's on sale but isn't normally cheap and grab it. And buy yourself a wine glass. Sure you may be a drunk, but you don't have to look it. And do NOT buy a box of wine. Wine is meant to be in bottles. Besides, throwing a box across the room in a drunken rage isn't nearly as fun.

Hard Alcohol

Again, let's not be buying the cheap stuff. You're better off trying to make your own rather than buying brands like Monarch. Monarch is for high school kids and street drunks. (If your finances demand you buy the cheap stuff, run it through a water purifier.)

Rum is Captain Morgan's or Bacardi. Or for rum you don't even need to mix, try Appleton Estates. Vodka is Skyy or depending on your tastes, Smirnoff. If you want top shelf vodka, I suggest Popov. Scotch is an acquired taste and different people like different things. If you don't know Scotch, get some Johnny Walker Black or any given 12-year-old single malt. For some of the best Scotch you'll ever taste, get someone with too much money to buy a bottle of Johnny Walker Blue. I don't like tequila so you're on your own there, but remember the clearer the tequila, the better it is.

Bars

This totally depends on what you like, but in my opinion you should have three bars that you frequent. Look around. Don't just pick the nearest bar to your place.

The first bar is a dive. The beer is cheap, vile, and plentiful. The crowd is the sort you see at your average bus stop or police line-up. This is the place to go when you look and feel like crap. It's also the place you go when you're low on cash. You order pitchers of beer, rarely come in without a friend, and drink quickly. Play darts and pool. Park close in case you need to leave in a hurry. The dive bar I go to is a place called The Unicorn where on one Friday night after last call, a Mexican pulled a knife on no one in particular and said, "What man or woman wants to go home with me tonight? I promise a night you won't forget." This brings up a point: Do not go home with anyone you meet here. You're better than that. Even when you're drunk.

The second bar is markedly better than the first. It has a better atmosphere, a full bar, and this is the most important part, a good bartender. This can't be stressed enough. A good bartender can turn a dive into a good bar. When you ask a good bartender for a Black Opal, he doesn't ask what's in it or say anything like, "It's not in the book." And if he can't make the drink you want, he suggests an adequate replacement. A good bartender asks you if you want another before you finish your drink. I could write another whole chapter on what makes a good bartender, but I think you get the point. Anyway, this is the bar you should spend the most time in and feel the most comfortable in. Order whatever mixed drink you like here that isn't easy to make at home. If you can't think of anything, get a White Russian with Irish Cream instead of milk. Get to know the people who work there. The better you know them, the better the service will be. It's okay to go home with people you meet here, but I don't suggest it. After all, they could be regulars too.

The third bar as you probably guessed, is a top-notch place. The sort of place you can afford to drink in, but need the plastic if you're going to eat. This place is reserved for dates you really like, low-key celebrations, and reminding yourself that you're not the sort of person who only drinks in dive bars. Order a Manhattan and enjoy it. It's a good drink and it lasts longer than most because you simply can't chug a Manhattan. You should not even try to pick up anyone here. This is a place you take people to impress them, but no one there will be impressed if you are alone.

Going on a Binge

Now that we have that out of the way, let's talk about Proper Drunk behavior. Proper Drunks know when to binge. The first thing to take into account is your location. You want to be as far away from people and places you deal with in everyday life as humanly possible. Try to be in another city or perhaps even an island.

When you're going for a binge drunk, it's best to load up a bit before you go out on the town and then go to a place you never plan on returning to. This makes it much easier for you to make a scene, get into a fight, or get into any other sort of trouble without ruining your reputation at your three bars. Bring a friend. Your friend can drink too, but he should not drink as much as you. He is there for crowd control and to explain your behavior to angry boyfriends and police officers if necessary. ("His wife left him yesterday and he got fired from his job this morning. Give him a break, man.") Drink a lot. And I mean enough to forget things. This is a binge and you should do it right. Besides, it helps to be telling the truth when someone confronts you and you respond with, "I don't remember."

Despite the success stories of people like Nick Nolte, Robert Downey Jr., and Hunter S. Thompson, for most of us, it is a good idea to limit your binge drinking to only once a month at most. Any more than that and it stops being a binge and becomes a lifestyle. There's not necessarily anything wrong with that, but you'll run out of friends who want to play zookeeper to your monkey behavior. It's best to reserve binges for the times in your life when a dumber person might commit suicide. Like when your parents die, or your marriage falls apart, or maybe a particularly bad Tuesday.

Recovery

Hey, who says you need to recover? If you drink on a regular basis and are okay with that, why stop? The body is a temple and temples are for defiling as much as for celebrations. The only time you need to worry about recovery is the morning after. This is why I recommend hangover-proof Skyy vodka. I once drank an entire bottle of Skyy and went to work at seven a.m. the next morning feeling great. (Sadly, the same cannot be said for that time I drank a bottle of Jameson.) Recovery is for people with drinking problems and as long as you don't have a problem with your drinking, you don't have to recover.

Being a Proper Drunk is not easy, but it's better than just being a drunk. And for some reason, it's a little more respectable. It's the details that matter. It's the difference between vomiting in a bar bathroom and vomiting on the bar. It may not seem like much, but ask any bartender, it's all the difference in the world.

Chapter 3

Stop Feeling Guilty

When I was in high school, I broke into my Earth Science classroom during lunch and found the final test. I copied down all the answers and sneaked out. Then when it came time for the test I wrote down all the answers and intentionally missed two just to make it look like I wasn't cheating. I told a friend of mine what I did and she said, "I could never do that. I'd feel so guilty."

Entire religions and societies have been built on the concept of guilt. If something bad happens, then the person responsible must feel guilty. People return found money. They refuse to take a bribe. Some people even decide not to have sex. And why? If you ask them, they'll tell you it's because of guilt. However, it isn't actually guilt that stops people from doing things. It is the fear of guilt. Sure you can say that there are all sorts of other reasons, but when you come down to it, you don't stray from your marriage because you're afraid you'll feel guilty. You don't rob a liquor store because of your fear of guilt. And it is your fear of guilt that stops you from ruining your life. Once you understand this, you are taking your first step to living a guilt free life. This is vital. Without learning to get rid of guilt, ruining your life is not only much more difficult, it's much less fun. And fun is your new God (along with Jesus of course. After all he is the most famous guy who didn't have a job, drank lots of wine with friends, and hung out with prostitutes. More on him later.)

We Have Nothing To Fear But....

From the time we are very young, we are told not to do things. We are told of the guilt we will have for doing bad things. Don't take an extra cookie from the cookie jar. Don't walk on the grass. Don't take drugs. Don't drive the car into the swimming pool. Along with these things, we are also told of things like Santa Claus and the Easter Bunny. Eventually we learn that all of this is really bullshit to make you behave. For some of us this revelation comes later than others. And there are some who spend their whole lives believing the lie of guilt.

You don't have to feel guilty and more importantly, you don't have to fear guilt.

Believing something makes it true. You believe you should feel guilt so you do. But consider this: Simple physics will tell you that a bullet cannot knock a man down. Bullets are too small to knock something the size of a man down, but time after time, people are shot and they instantly fall down. The reason they fall down is that they believe they are supposed to fall down. It is the same thing with guilt. You only feel guilt after doing something 'wrong' because you think you're supposed to.

Guilty Conscience

This is not an easy thing to overcome. And there are reasons for this. Guilt is the last way your parents or any other authority figure has to control you. By instilling you with guilt over certain actions, your parents, your government, your church, your significant other, or whoever else, has exerted a certain amount of control over your actions, over your behavior, and over who you are.

But let's get real here, the only time you want someone exerting control over you is when you're handcuffed to a bed during semi-kinky sex. You need to be yourself, not what everyone else wants you to be. It's time to free yourself from these bonds of guilt. Fight Club was wrong. It is not after losing everything that you're free to do anything. It is after you lose your fear of guilt.

Guilt Free Living

And how do you lose your fear of guilt? The same way an actor is able to become his part; by knowing your motivation. It's hard to feel bad for doing something when you know why you did it. I cheated on my science test because I needed a good grade and I didn't study. To me that was a good reason. Sure, there are those who would say I deserved to fail but they're the same people who live by their own fear of guilt, but as I'm sure you've discovered, this world does not operate by what people deserve. I mean cheating on your spouse is one thing, but it's another thing if you cheat on your spouse who drinks every night and calls you by the wrong name in bed. For everything you do there is a reason for it. As long as you can understand those reasons, your fear of guilt and guilt itself will disappear. Remember, a good enough reason is what turns homicide into justifiable homicide.

Once you can do this, your actions are truly your own. Without the shadow of guilt hanging over everything you do, you'll find you smile more often and doubt much less. Trust me, ruining your life is much easier when you don't feel bad about doing it. Guilt is for those who cannot govern themselves. Are you so weak that you must live in fear of guilt for the rest of your life? I didn't think so. It is time to become an adult and get rid of that last bit of childishness. There is no Santa Claus, Easter Bunny, or guilt. Of course, when the time comes though, there's no reason to tell your kids that.

Chapter 4

Drive Like A Maniac

I've been in twenty-six car accidents. I've been in cars that have flown through the air and tumbled into swamps and sunk. I've had two cars explode. I've driven a sparkle blue '66 Impala and a brand new Ferrari. Once a friend of mine said, "Jack, I want you to teach me to drive." I was surprised and asked him why he didn't know how to drive. He said, "Oh, I know how to drive. I want to know how to drive like you." Well, here's a crash course in driving like me.

Know Your Wheels

First, you must know your vehicle. All of it. Everything from the tire pressure to the kind of motor you have to what's in the trunk. You need to know how fast you can take a corner and at what point the tires give. You need to know how fast you can stop and how fast you can accelerate again. You need to know what the top speed of your vehicle really is. And the only way to know all these things is to practice.

Take your car out to the biggest parking lot you can find between 3am and 5am and see what your motherfucker's got. Practice skidding to a halt and cornering in an area where screwing up isn't likely to wreck your car. You'll want to time yourself and do this no longer than ten or fifteen minutes. Sooner or later some insomniac neighbor will call the cops and it's best to not be around when that happens. Don't worry. There's always tomorrow night.

Between 3am and 5am is the best time to test out your car because that's when the fewest vehicles are on the road. Driving like a maniac doesn't mean driving dangerously. It simply means appearing out of control while having complete control. A real maniac driver is able to be completely calm while the other people in the car freak the fuck out. The only way to get that calm is to know what you and your vehicle are truly capable of.

Know Your Enemy

I once saw a local cop who liked to do stand-up comedy. One of his best jokes was, "I pull people over and they say, 'Why aren't you going after murderers and drug dealers and rapists?' And I'd say, 'Because I'll get fuckin' shot! That's why.'" This is true. Most cops would rather bust you for a moving violation because they're less likely to get hurt. This means that more than anything else I might mention in this book, driving like a maniac is a good way to get some face time with the boys and girls in blue…Unless you watch out.

Be aware of on ramps and overpasses where cops might hang out. Be on the lookout for dark sedans or exempt license plates. Better yet, find a patsy. The best car to be on the road is the second fastest car. If you're going 80mph, find the guy going 90mph. He's the one they'll bust. Cops go for the easy mark, so don't make it easy. Having a car that isn't a bright color is also a good idea. It's kind of easy to find a bright red Ferrari whereas a tan Nissan Altima looks like every other car on the road. Should you find a cop behind you, the best thing to do is take no more than two corners, pull over, get out of the car, and walk up to the nearest house. Knock on the door and ask directions to somewhere. Do anything to take some time for the cop to disappear.

Note: Do NOT try this trick if they've already turned their lights on.

Know Your Terrain

This is arguably the most important thing about driving like a maniac. Be aware of your surroundings at all times. Don't drive crazy fast on a road unless you know it. Pay attention to the road conditions. If the roads are wet and it hasn't rained in a while there will be more oil on the roads and they'll be a bit slicker.

Knowing your environment though doesn't just extend to roads. You also want to pay close attention to the other cars on the road. This doesn't mean just knowing where the cars are, but also where they're going to be. Look for potential openings and exits.

Know Your Limits

There is a limit to how fast every car can go without being entirely unstable. There's also a limit to how fast a road can be driven down realistically. Being aware of these limits makes driving like a maniac not only a lot safer, it also makes it a lot easier. The limits are usually higher than most people think they are and ruining your life is all about finding these limits. The unfortunate thing is that most of the time the way to find a limit is to go just a bit beyond it.

Should you manage to wrap your car around a pole, you're going to need a tow truck. I highly suggest having a tow truck company in mind. It helps if you get to know a tow truck driver. Call them up to get their rates. Get a card from them. You look a hell of a lot more responsible if there's already a tow truck on the way when the cops arrive.

All in all, driving like a maniac can be a hell of a lot of fun and a much more interesting way to get from Point A to Point B. Ruining your life is living life in the fast lane and the best way to do that is with the pedal to the floor. Good luck.

Chapter 5

Make It Work For The Story

There was a time when I really didn't care about much of anything and I tended to do a lot of stupid things, like sleep with people I didn't know and get really drunk and/or high every night. During this time, the only way I kept anything straight was by writing down everything that happened each day and reading it the next morning to figure out what I did. It was also during that time that I came up with a new philosophy on life.

When going on a bender you need to be able to make morally ambiguous decisions quickly. Is it a good idea to have another drink? Should you steal that car? Do you really want to help your friend hide that body? Eventually I came up with a system to answer these questions. This system consisted of three questions. Add to these questions one rule and you will have a philosophy on life that I guarantee will make your life interesting in the Chinese sense of the word.

Question One: Is It Right?

Generally speaking you can tell if a decision is right or wrong. It's just a matter of how right or wrong. Hitting someone for no reason? Wrong. Hitting someone with a reason? Less Wrong. Hitting someone for a good reason? Righteous. Odds are you can figure this one out if you really think about it. And if you can't, well that's why we have three questions and not just one, which brings us to…

Question Two: Is It Legal?

So you've figured out if it's right and maybe it is, but is it legal? Is it something you could do in front of a cop without having to run afterwards? Often the legality of something depends on the state you're in (and occasionally the age of the other people involved). In some states, oral sex is still outlawed. But just because it's illegal doesn't make it wrong. The reason for this question is because illegal activities have potentially bad consequences, like prison and lawyer's bills. If it isn't legal, you may want to take some precautionary measures to avoid getting caught. (And should you get caught, please refer to Chapter 9 'Talk to Cops', and Chapter 10 'Get Arrested'.) Once you have answered question two, you can move on to…

Question Three: Does It Work For The Story?

It might not be right. It might not even be legal. But it just might make a great story. For example, meeting a seventeen-year-old at a party and sleeping with her two hours later isn't right, and depending on how old you are and where you are, it may not be legal. However, something like that makes a great story. (I'm just using this as a hypothetical situation. It's not as if I have any personal experience with something like this. No, really.) Great stories are one of the reasons we are alive. We don't want to live vicariously through movies. We want to have our own adventures. And the best way to do this is to be aware of the story.

We all have the story of our lives but it is up to us to make sure that story is worth telling. No one wants to hear about how you graduated from college, got a good job, worked 9 to 5 for 30 years and retired. They want to hear about how you cheated on your college tests, stole money from the company, and had sex with the boss's daughter. All work and no morally ambiguous situations makes Jack a dull boy.

Now with these three questions in mind, we must think about

The Rule: If The Answer To Question Three Is "Yes.", Disregard The First Two Questions And Do It.

I realize there are people who will think you can just use question three, but for some reason that doesn't work as well. You need to have the first two questions. I don't know why. That's just how it is. If you just use question three, bad things will happen. Things that tend to make it unlikely you'll be around to tell the story. Just trust me on this.

This philosophy will not win you friends or make you rich, but it will almost guarantee you have a good time.

One last note: After some pretty good stories, I've learned that there is a fourth question that should be asked.

Question Four: If It Might Kill Me, Will It Make A Good Last Chapter?

Death makes everything a lot less fun. (Usually anyway.) This is why this is a good question to keep in mind and a dangerous one to leave out. You want to ruin your life, not end it. If it isn't going to kill you, then just refer to the first three questions and the rule.

However, just because it might kill you doesn't mean you shouldn't do it. If that were the case, no one would go bungee jumping or listen to The Cure. What you want to do is make sure it makes a good last chapter. I mean nothing sucks more than a good story with a bad ending. Another thing to keep in mind is that you need witnesses so someone can write this last chapter. This is why JFK had a great last chapter: Lots of witnesses.

So there you have it. A personal philosophy on life that's easier to remember than the Ten Commandments and faster than the I-Ching. Use these words of wisdom as your personal guide for life and....well, God only knows what might happen. One thing's for sure though, you'll be living in interesting times.

Chapter 6

Tell Lies

In the course of ruining your life, you will undoubtedly end up in a position where you should lie. The truth is occasionally not something everyone needs to know. The thing is that you need to learn how to lie correctly. Lying is the art of creating absolute bullshit out of thin air. There are many ways to do this and since this book shows you quite a few ways to get into trouble, it seems only fair that I show you one of the best ways to get out of it.

WHAT YOU SHOULD NOT DO:

Let's start off by talking about the bad ways to lie. Ironically enough these are the most common lies. For some reason, when it comes to lying, even the smartest people end up telling the dumbest lies.

Outright Denial

I didn't do it. Whatever it is, it isn't my fault. I have no clue what you're talking about. These phrases do not work unless they are true. And even then denial sounds more than a little like bullshit. Denying something is the easiest way to get caught lying. Ask Bill Clinton. More often than not, anyone accusing you of anything has some sort of evidence to back it up. If you just deny that something happened, it just proves to them that it did.

Alibi Lying

This is the classic "Jim, if Lisa asks where I was last night, tell her I was with you." lie. The idea that if you involve more people in a lie it is more believable only works if those people know how to lie and can keep the lie to themselves. You should never do this because there is no reason for you to believe anyone will actually back you up. For all you know, Jim wants Lisa to find out because he's got a thing for her. Lying is a delicate thing and delicate things are best done alone.

Repeated Lying

This is where you tell a dumb lie ("I didn't do it.") and then try to cover it up with a slightly less dumb lie ("I don't think I did it.") and when that doesn't work you use yet another dumb lie ("I didn't mean to do it.") This never ever works. And if you are guilty of this sort of lying at all, then you need to be very careful how you lie in the future. Every discovered lie makes you less trustworthy and makes it more difficult for you to lie effectively. And as strange as it sounds, this sort of thing actually makes it harder to tell the truth. I'll give you a personal example: I spent the night at this one girl's apartment and all we did was drink, smoke, and talk. We did not so much as touch each other. Coming home and trying to tell my girlfriend at the time that nothing happened was not easy. Due to telling dumb lies in the past, she had many reasons not to believe me even though I was actually telling the truth.

WHAT YOU SHOULD DO:

Now that we've gotten those out of the way, let's talk about the right ways to lie.

Provable Lies

This may seem like an oxymoron but it isn't. Often evidence can be used to point to the wrong conclusion. Ask OJ. All you have to do is create evidence that supports your lie. If you have evidence of your own to back up whatever you say, it will get you a hell of a lot further than just words. A book of matches from whatever bar you say you were at. Details of the movie you were supposedly seeing. Ticket stubs to a show you didn't go to. Anything at all that makes your lie seem true. This is actually a lot easier than it sounds.

Given the right evidence, people tend to assume the truth of your words. After all, if you can prove your lie, who's to say it isn't true?

Incidentally this is one of the reasons why it's best not to have any unique traits like bright pink hair or a neck tattoo. If someone happens to see you in a place you're not supposed to be you want it to at least be possible that it wasn't you.

80% Truth

The most important thing about lying is that you believe your own lie. If you don't believe what you're saying, why should anyone else? This is why it's a good idea to make sure that every lie you tell has around 80% truth to it. For example, let's say you have sex with someone you shouldn't have. Your significant other is probably more intuitive than you think but the last thing you want to say is the truth so a conversation with 80% truth might go like this:

"Where were you last night?"

"I'll tell you the truth. I was out with Linda."

Now admitting that you were exactly where she suspects makes the upcoming lies easier to believe because the most obvious thing to lie about is who you were with. It's also the easiest thing to get caught lying about. This is why you might as well tell the truth. Let's continue:

"What?!? So, what did you and Linda do last night?"

"Nothing much."

A good ambiguous answer, but it's not going to get you anywhere in a situation like this:

"What do you mean by 'nothing much'?"

"Well, we were drinking and one thing led to another and, uh, well, we kissed."

You should not leave it at that. You should ramble on a bit more but not admit anything else. Talk until she interrupts you. After she finishes yelling or whatever, you say this:

"We kissed, okay? I'm sorry. I screwed up. I hope you can find some way to forgive me. I now realize how much I really love you. Blah. Blah. Blah."

Sure, this is more than you wanted to admit, but it's also more than she would expect you to admit, which will make it all that much more believable that all you did was kiss.

Please note: Lying like this is NOT a good idea when being questioned by the police. (See Chapter 9 Talk to the Cops) Admitting to lesser offenses in the presence of police officers is a bad idea because you might not be aware of what a lesser offense is. For example in the state of Maryland admitting to being an accomplice to a murder will get you just as much time as doing the murder itself.

Omitting

That little hypothetical situation leads to the next great way to lie: omission. This is a favorite of politicians because technically you aren't lying. Come to think of it the Linda story is more an example of omission than 80% truth. Sorry about that. Still, omission is the best possible way to lie. You don't say, "I didn't do it." That is an outright lie. You just neglect to mention what you did. If someone comes right out and directly asks you a question like, "Did you have sex with Linda?" You'll have to go back to the 80% truth thing and say, "We kissed a little." Again, you aren't really lying here. You are actually telling the truth. You did kiss her. The nice part about answers like this is that it seems like you answered the question but you didn't. This way if she finds out the truth you can say, "I never said I *didn't* have sex with her."

However, don't expect this to get you off the hook. We'll discuss the truth in the next chapter.

'Forgetting'

Now as long as we're talking about ways that politicians lie, let's talk about 'forgetting'. Pretending to not remember something is the easiest way to lie because no one can prove that you do remember. The phrase you are looking for is, "I have no recollection of that." Or "I don't remember that." These are phrases that may make you look stupid, but it is better to be considered stupid than evil. Ask anyone in the Bush family.

It's also good to back this up by pretending to forget random things from time to time. Having a reputation for having a bad memory can be a really good thing if you're up to no good.

Paper Trail

Any cop will tell you that people leave evidence of where they were and what they did all the time. Receipts. Cell phone bills. Witnesses. Mileage inconsistencies. A stamp on the back of your hand. If you're going to lie, you need to cover up any evidence that contradicts your story. Regardless of how good you lie, a receipt from the wrong bar can ruin it all.

Whenever you're doing something shady use cash, pay phones, and nondescript clothing. It's okay to dress well, just not too well. Fit in to your surroundings. And if you happen to have a flashy car, don't use it. If you treat it like you're robbing a bank and get as paranoid as a criminal, then you can get away with a lot provided you don't leave a trail for anyone to follow.

Reality Check

It would be irresponsible of me to write a chapter on lying without mentioning that you really should lie as little as possible. The more you lie, no matter how well, the more likely you will get caught and while you may be trying to ruin your life, if you ask me, it's better to ruin your life honestly. When you lie, you need to make sure that it is a quick and easy lie that will need no support in the future. You don't want to say that you were away in the Army Reserves last weekend when that means you'll have to disappear two weekends a month from then on (unless of course, you want to be able to disappear two weekends a month). The ability to lie effectively is invaluable. A good liar is someone who seems to never lie. Which brings us to the end of this chapter and the beginning of the next.

Chapter 7

Tell The Truth

Okay. Now that you know how to lie, let's talk about telling the truth. It sounds a lot simpler than it is. The truth is an elusive thing. As soon as you start talking about it, you get further away from what it is. Try asking anyone to define the truth and they'll either lie to you or get a headache trying to tell you what it is. Honesty is not always the best policy and it isn't something that the average person is very familiar with. Just about everyone has a public relations section of their brain that polishes things up before they say them. You certainly don't want to say, "Last night I had sex with your sister." Instead you might say, "Oh, by the way, I saw your sister yesterday." There are mental filters that stop the average person so they can get along in society without upsetting too many people no matter how bad their actual behavior might be. This is why it's so hard for cops to get a confession from a killer.

However, this book is not about getting along in society and not offending or upsetting people. This book is called Ruin Your Life for a reason. It's time to be honest. Sure, if you read the last chapter, you can lie better than Bill Clinton after a bachelor party, but the ability to lie is like the ability to fire a gun: it's extremely useful to know how to do it but no one wants to be around someone who does it all the time. You should lie only when absolutely necessary. This not only makes your lying more effective, it also makes your life simpler. Life is easy when you don't have to remember too many lies.

"You Can Handle The Truth!"

There is no reason in the world to lie about your past. No matter what you did, let it out. I had sex with a sixteen-year old when I was twenty-one, cheated on my fiancé with an ex-girlfriend, burned my high school chemistry teacher's grade book, and did more drugs than most people think I have. I've gotten an entire bar to chant, "Kill yourself!" to this guy I didn't even know. I watched a fatal car wreck happen and made a joke about it as I drove by. And the best part is that I didn't have to make any of that up. I don't have to hide it or hope no one finds out. And my friends and enemies end up knowing the real me. I don't hide anything from anyone. I have no secrets at all and I'm proud of that. The fact that anyone can ask me any question and I don't have to worry about my answer is very comforting.

I know it can be hard to let go of secrets and stop hiding behind alibis and made up stories, but it's also very liberating. The easiest way to avoid skeletons being found in your closet is to keep them out in the open for all to see. No one can betray you by exposing a secret if you have none. They can tell anyone anything about you and you don't have to worry.

Not everyone can do this. For some this approach to life is simply too dangerous. A report from the Vatican released in 2001 says that priests have been having sex with and in some cases raping nuns as well as forcing them to get abortions. This is clearly horrible behavior and you won't see me condoning it, but this wouldn't have happened if they didn't hide their desires. It would have been out in the open and the offending priests would have been sent to seedy singles bars where they belong.

No one said telling the truth is easy. What you have to do is act like a good reporter. Just tell the facts and let whoever hears you judge for themselves. Don't try to explain it or polish it up so it looks better than it is. Just say, "I did it!" Who cares what other people think? I've always told people, "If you don't like the truth, change it, but don't get pissed off at me when I say it." If you don't like that people call you an alcoholic, stop drinking. If you don't like being poor, rob a bank or marry up. These are simple concepts.

This will not win you friends. This will not make you popular. It probably won't even get you laid. But it will make you right. And it's really nice to be right especially if you're doing something wrong. The best part is that the people who decide to hate you don't actually hate you. They hate the truth. Granted, they probably won't pay attention to this difference but it's still an important one.

"Yes, you're fat."

"No, I wasn't listening."

"No, we can't just be friends."

"Yes, there is someone else, three someones actually."

"I don't know if I love you and I don't think I'll ever really know."

"Yes, I'm a hypocrite."

"No, there were never any weapons of mass destruction."

"I don't remember or care how much I had to drink tonight. I want another."

"No, I wasn't actually working late."

"Yes, I know where the body is buried."

The list goes on and on. Telling the truth makes you the biggest jerk in the world, but you will be a righteous jerk. Ultimately all you are doing is saying something honest. If they don't like it, well that's their problem, not yours.

Chapter 8

Write It Down

I started writing things that weren't homework assignments in the third grade. And with the exception of three years in the mid-nineties when I went insane, I've been writing ever since. When I was sixteen, I started keeping a journal. I would continue on the history of my writing but by now you're probably wondering what the hell any of this has to do with ruining your life. I mean that is the purpose of this book. I run around telling people if I make just one life a little more interesting, I've done my job. Well, from here on out, it gets a bit darker. So far I've been talking about things I regard as fun and games. Now it's time to get serious. If you aren't ready for it, burn this book. (I can't make any money off it if you sell it on eBay.)

Keep A Journal

Okay, for starters, if you haven't already, you need to start keeping a journal. This may not seem like a big thing, but trust me, it's the most important thing you'll do. When you have finally ruined your life, when you have destroyed everything you're supposed to work for, when you finally realize that one day you won't be around to torment those people you can't stand, when on one fateful night you fall to your knees in tears wondering how it ever came to this, you will be happy you kept a journal. And it will be that if nothing else that you will be thankful for.

Immortalize Yourself

Oh, sure you might not like what you write and maybe it turns out that you suck as a writer, so what. It doesn't matter. What matters is that once you write it down, people can read it. As you read these words keep in mind that it's entirely possible that I am dead. I could have written this book, sent it off to the publishers, walked outside and got hit by a Dodge Dart driven by my ex-wife, or maybe the crab meat I bought at the store an hour ago isn't as fresh as they say it is and I eat it and drop dead. Or maybe my heart will just stop beating for no reason at all and I will die a medical mystery. Any of these things could happen and you could still read this tomorrow. Writing is immortal and that's why I love it. And that's why you must keep a journal. Because if you're going to ruin your life, you need to let others know why or at the very least how, you did it. You need to show them that you weren't crazy at all. Or maybe you were, but at least you were literate.

Read Your Own Story

Write it down. This isn't just for posterity or for other people. It's for YOU. If you do the things suggested in this book, you will wake up on more than one occasion with no memory of the previous night. You will wonder what the hell you were thinking at the time. You will not find any of these answers unless you write them down.

Keep in mind that I'm not really trying to help. I am only telling you the right way to do the wrong things. I am giving you the tools to live a life that will be worth living, but not worth anything else. If you do everything I tell you to, you will not be popular. You will not be rich. You will not even have much more sex than the next person. I make no guarantees at all. If you need advice, talk to Dear Abby. If you need *a* vice, talk to me.

When it has all fallen down, you can look at the journal and see how you got where you are. When they ask how it all happened, give them the journal. Only by writing it down, will you ever really know what your mindset was at that time. Over the last few months I've been transcribing my journals onto my computer and I have been amazed at what I wrote. Not because the writing is incredible, but because it tells a story that in parts I don't even really remember. I have written in my journal while drunk, stoned, injured, and on a couple occasions all three and while, to be honest, my journals have gotten me into trouble from time to time, I have never once regretted writing it all down.

Chapter 9

Talk To Cops

Cops. In the course of ruining your life, you are bound to encounter the men and women of law enforcement. Not all of these encounters will be pleasant. Police officers are not known for their sense of humor or tolerance. And while it may seem that getting arrested is an excellent way to ruin your life, you should try to avoid prison for as long as possible. Drugs, sex, and all other forms of fun are considerably more costly and significantly of lower quality in prison.

Don't worry about those mean boys and girls in blue. I am here to help you (well not really, but this once let's pretend I am). Cops can be dealt with and I happen to know a couple things about talking to cops. One time a cop pulled me over and arrested me for having a suspended license. Though I was handcuffed in the back of the car and had been advised that I could remain silent, I still talked to him. Fifteen minutes later, he dropped me off at my apartment and told me how I could apply to be a cop. Dealing with the police is just like putting up a website: once you know a couple of basic things, it's easy.

Let's start off by pointing out mistakes many people make. These are the most common things people do and they hardly ever work. For examples of these, feel free to watch any given episode of Cops.

WHAT YOU SHOULD NOT DO:

Don't Play Innocent

The phrase cops hear more than any other is, "I didn't do it." They hear it so often that they just ignore it on general principle. Of course you aren't innocent. If you were innocent, the cops wouldn't be there and they sure as hell wouldn't be talking to you. You or someone in your near vicinity must have done something. Unless you can point to a better suspect and hopefully have some sort of proof, playing innocent isn't going to work.

Don't Get Angry

This seems almost too obvious, but for some reason there are a lot of people out there who think that yelling at a cop will help the situation. Ask yourself this, would you want to help someone who is yelling at you or would you throw the book at the fucker? That's right.

Human nature answers anger with anger and the last thing you want is an angry cop. Remember angry people do stupid things. And at the end of the day the judge will believe the cop over you. So stay calm.

Don't Get Technical

There's a reason there are so many lawyer jokes. No one likes them. Quoting law to a cop is like quoting the bible to a missionary. Odds are the cop knows the law better than you and what little you might know about unlawful searches is nothing compared to what the cop might know about 'necessary force'. Beat the cops in court, not on the street.

Don't Run

Have you ever seen a cop let a guy go after he runs? Me neither. A friend of mine who is an ex-cop told me that he and his friends have a rule, "If you make us run, we make you pay."

I used to have a job transcribing police reports and sentences like "Suspect apparently fell on concrete during arrest and lost a few teeth" were a lot more common on the runners than anyone else and I doubt it was because they were clumsy.

WHAT YOU SHOULD DO:

Okay, so we're clear on what not to do. Now let me tell you what works. Keep in mind that when I say it works, I mean it works most of the time. Sometimes you're going to run into cops who just want to bust you no matter what. And sometimes the circumstances of your situation make talking your way out of it almost impossible. These situations are usually easy to spot. Bodies, bloody clothing, or large quantities of drugs are a dead giveaway. If you notice that there is no way to talk your way out of it, do the smart thing and shut up. The only English words you know at that point are, "I want a lawyer."

However, more often than not, you can talk your way out of it. Cops are like you and me. They don't want to do any more than they absolutely have to. Arresting you makes for a lot more paperwork than a written warning. So here are some pointers that have worked for me in the past.

Cops Are People Too

If you treat a cop like a real person you'll get a lot further than you would treating him like a uniform. This is his job. He works a shift just like you. A cop spends most of his time dealing with the sort of people you try to avoid sitting near on the bus. What he wants more than anything else is to meet someone who is just a good person. Be that bright spot in the cop's day. The second you start treating him like just a cop is the second he starts treating you like just a criminal. Be friendly. And I don't mean bullshit friendly. I mean genuine didn't-I-go-to-high-school-with-you friendly. As if this is someone you might go out for a drink with. The second you start treating him like an adversary, he'll respond accordingly.

It's Just A Misunderstanding

Cops arrest criminals. If they can't find a crime, they won't arrest anyone. When a cop confronts you, you should appear relieved by his presence. Finally, someone is here to help you sort out this misunderstanding. This should not be confused with the 'innocent' defense. Surely something was done. But it wasn't what it appears.

Once I was throwing a party for a friend who was joining the Navy. He was just out of high school and honestly I was one of three people there who were of legal drinking age. There were well over fifty people at the party. The entire girls swim team from the local high school had arrived direct from state championship. When the cops showed up, high school kids went running out the back door. A couple of them were smoking joints as fast as they could, trying to get high and get rid of evidence at the same time. There wasn't one sober person there. I was quite drunk myself, but I managed to coherently answer the door. They asked if someone in a gray Honda had been here. I had no idea, but if they're asking, it's probably true.

"Yes, what's this all about, officer?" (Sounding as concerned as possible.) The two cops proceeded to tell me how neighbors heard these hooligans in the Honda yelling obscenities and generally disturbing the peace. I instantly picked up on this. They aren't after me, just some fuckheads in a Honda. The thing to do was make their enemy my own: "Oh yeah, I remember those punks." I continued to lie my ass off as I told them this story of a Honda full of high school kids coming into the party and trying to grab some beer.

"But I kicked them out because they were underage. I bet that's why they were yelling, officer." As I said this, there were teenagers peeking through the blinds directly to the right of the oblivious cops.

"I'm sorry for the misunderstanding, officers. Have a good night." And that was that.

Friends On The Force

It always helps to have friends in positions of authority. If you have a friend who is a cop, make sure you drop his name. Don't expect this to get you off exclusively, but it could very well start you on that road away from the back of the squad car. If you don't have any police officer friends, get some. Go to your local police station and ask to go on a ride along. Knowing the cop who shows up is the best possible way to avoid a ticket or getting arrested. Thanks to my former job in police records and having gone on a few ride alongs, I happen to know more than a couple of people on the force here in Tacoma. This has helped me on more than one occasion.

As I said before, these techniques will not always work. It depends on the attitude of the cop, the circumstances of the situation, and your skill at talking your way out of things. We'll talk about what to do when all else fails in the next chapter.

Good luck.

Chapter 10

Get Arrested

Despite multiple restraining orders, two arrest warrants, a suspended driver's license, and a lot of really bad choices, I've managed to get arrested only once. During the time I was in jail, I thought to myself how one day I could write about it and I wouldn't hate the fact I was there. Turns out I was half right.

So what happens when all the stuff I told you in the last chapter doesn't work? What happens when you've actually screwed up enough that the cops just can't ignore it? Or perhaps the cops are just pricks and want to arrest you just for the hell of it. And if you happen to be naïve enough to think that doesn't happen, let me just say that once when I went on a ride along, the cop said, "Well, it's a Monday afternoon, so it'll be slow, but I'll try to arrest someone and make it fun for ya." You can get arrested for just about anything nowadays and when it happens, it's best to be prepared.

You Have The Right To Remain Silent

There's a reason you're told this. Cops don't want to do any more work than they have to. If you just shut the hell up after they arrest you, then they can file their little report, drop you off for processing, and be done with you.

That's assuming that all you did was some minor crime. If you're looking at more major crimes, such as homicide, the right to remain silent isn't just a good idea, it's about the only thing in the world that might save your psychotic ass. When you are arrested, the only thing you should be saying to the cops is, "I want a lawyer." You should say this early and as often as possible if you are actually being questioned. Keep in mind that cops don't charge you and for the most part, they don't really give a damn if you're guilty or innocent. The only thing cops have to do is present the case to the prosecutor and if they've gone to the trouble of arresting you, they will want every piece of evidence you can give them. This includes that bullshit story you think is the perfect alibi. Instead, give them nothing. Under no circumstances should you talk about the crime with anyone at all without your lawyer present.

Cops are notorious for trying to get around this. If they're really wanting to talk to you, they'll tell you your lawyer is late or they'll say that you don't need a lawyer and it's just a few questions. The only reason you have been arrested is to be charged with a crime. No matter how friendly they might be, you should realize that these people are not your friends. Their job is to lock people up. So many criminals help themselves into long prison sentences by talking to the cops after it's already too late. Once those cuffs are on, it's best to let any talking to the cops be done by your attorney.

One Phone Call

No matter what you tell them, once you're in that holding cell, the only way you're getting out of jail is bail. In most jails, there will be something right next to the phone that lists all the local bail bonds companies. Don't call them unless you have no one else to call. What you want to do is call your best friend. Though it might not have sunken in at this point, you are locked in a cage. You need someone on the outside doing everything possible to get you out of this cage. This is the person who will call the bail bonds company, get the money together, and pick your ass up when bail is posted at midnight on a Wednesday.

When I was arrested, they sent me over to the phone and I made my call. I wanted to finish it as quickly as possible so my best friend could get to work getting me out. Then, since no one was really paying attention, I made another call to another friend. This call, more than anything else, was made simply to keep me on the phone as long as possible. The thing to remember is that this is your last contact with the outside world for God only knows how long. Talk on the phone until they tell you to stop. Even if no one is on the line. Every second you spend on the phone is a second you're not in the holding cell.

The Holding Cell

Jails differ from city to city. A jail in Chicago is not going to be the same as a jail in Ely, Nevada. However, generally speaking, the first form of jail you will encounter after they fingerprint you, take your mug shot, and give you your jail clothes is the holding cell. This is where they will keep you until they can transfer you to the proper jail.

Holding cells are interesting places. Everyone in a holding cell woke up in the morning a free man and then had a really bad fucking day. People react differently to this sort of thing. Most are pissed as hell and odds are, so are you. Keep in mind that the one thing you have in common with these people is your sudden hatred for cops. If you feel like talking to your cellmates, "Those fucking cops." is a good icebreaker. No one is going to argue with that.

You may actually get along with the people in the holding cell. If so, good, but keep in mind that these guys are not your friends either. If you have a brain in your head, they will never be your friends. There's no reason to tell them one little piece of truthful information about your life. After all, the nice guy sitting across from you may be there for breaking into friends' houses and carving his name on their backs. These guys are criminals not buddies.

Jail

If they transfer you to the jail, odds are that your friend has failed to come up with the bail in a timely manner. You're probably there for the night. They will give you a blanket, a cup, a toothbrush, and some toothpaste. Once it is night, they will turn out the lights expecting for some reason that you're actually going to be able to sleep in a room with twenty to thirty other criminals.

The thing to do is take the toothbrush and put the bristle end in the palm of your hand with the handle sticking out. This is the closest thing to a weapon you're likely to find and it will go in someone's eye easily. I know this sounds harsh, but for those of you who don't know, people die in jails. Often for no reason at all and honestly the cops barely care if some criminal is dumb enough to get killed. The real statistics of violence in city jails is truly scary. The only thing scarier is how many people really don't care that it happens. Unless you're the mayor's kid, odds are they will just chalk it up to bad luck for the 'newbie'.

Bail

Hopefully, you will make bail and you will have a best friend who you will owe for life. Being bailed out is the best feeling in the world. You suddenly realize that there are people out there who give a flying fuck whether or not you're incarcerated even after all the shit you've put them through. I'm talking from personal experience, but I think that the feeling is the same for everyone.

Contrary to what you might think, getting arrested is not a good way to ruin your life. It isn't fun. It isn't interesting. And everyone in the place is the sort of person you try to stay away from in daily life. However, if you are actually trying to ruin your life and not just reading this for a laugh, then there is a good chance you will get arrested and it seems only fair that I help you out with advice since you can't count on me for bail.

Chapter 11

Eat The Last Cookie

Ruining your life is about being irresponsible. It's about doing what you want to do when you want to do it. It's about savoring every aspect of life. When you get right down to it, I daresay it's all about cookies. I know it sounds crazy but hear me out on this. There is no cookie more important than the Last Cookie.

I saw a comedian years ago that helped me come up with what I like to refer to as Last Cookie Theory. Calling something a theory always adds weight to it. It sounds like there has been testing and such. This is why I don't call it "What I Know About Cookies".

The theory is fairly simple: Imagine you're eating a plate of cookies and watching television. It's a movie in which one of your favorite actresses gets naked or so you heard. Though you've also heard it's a quick scene. Despite the fact that you are a fairly well educated intelligent sort, you still want that possible glimpse of nipple. So you munch away at your plate of cookies without looking.

Your hand reaches down to the plate as the actress says she's going to take a shower, but to your surprise, there are no more cookies. You look down to confirm it and miss the scene. But more important than that is the fact that you've just eaten the last cookie without getting the 'Last Cookie Sensation'.

By now, I'm sure you're wondering what a plate of cookies has to do with ruining your life. This is where the application of the Last Cookie Theory comes in. Think back on one of your favorite relationships. Do you remember the last time you had sex with this person? If you do, I'll bet that at the time you had no idea it was going to be the last time you two were going to have sex. That's just how it works most of the time. And the problem with this is that you never get that 'Last Cookie Sensation'. Your plate is empty and all you can do is try to find more cookies and when you find them, you're probably going to eat the last cookie again without ever knowing it.

How To Eat The Last Cookie

Here's the thing. With the 'Last Sex Cookie', you aren't the only one eating. This means you're going to have to be a little deceptive. Since I've already covered how to lie, this should be no problem.

You do NOT want to say anything like, "Well, let's do it one more time for old time's sake." That rarely, if ever works, and if you happen to be with someone that does work on, please move onto the next chapter and send me her number.

What you want to do is pretend that everything is going fine in the relationship. Let it just happen the way it's always happened. But this time, you will be aware that it's the Last Time. Congratulations, the Last Cookie Sensation is yours.

Sharing The Last Cookie

So you're going to have your Last Sex Cookie, but while your partner might not be aware it's the last cookie, there is still every reason to share it with them. This is it. This is the finale. You want this to be the time they remember. This means being attentive and not just going in for the quick fuck. Go out of your way to make it long, slow, and meaningful. There's no reason for this to be a bad or short memory for either of you. Cookies are happy things.

The best part about sharing the cookie is that if you share enough, there may be a chance for more cookies. And when you realize your plate is empty, the thing you want more than anything else is more cookies.

Other Cookies

So far I've only talked about the Last Sex Cookie. Definitely a good cookie, but there are other Last Cookies in life. The Last Day At Work Cookie. The Last Time in Your Apartment Cookie. The Last Time You Rob A Bank Cookie. These are things to savor, but you can only do that if you pay attention to the number of cookies on the plate.

The Last Cookie Sensation may not seem like a big deal but remember making things work for the story? Well the story needs some sort of completion. And it's just not complete without that Last Cookie Sensation.

Chapter 12

Dare To Not Care

Everyone has heard about the wonderful exhilaration that you get when you fall in love. It is a liberating feeling that makes you think anything is possible and that the whole world is yours. Every day is built for you. Even bad things hardly bother you. What few people realize is that this same feeling occurs at another point in life: when you realize that you just don't care.

Apathy Now!

The ability to not care is both a gift and a skill. All of a sudden it doesn't matter if your significant other is working late or screwing a coworker. News of an airplane crash doesn't bother you. You stop wondering when your girlfriend is going to call. You can be nice when you want to be nice and mean when you want to be mean because when it comes right down to it, you just don't care.

Let me tell you a story about my buddy, Nate. One night he went home with this cute bartender. They had your typical one night stand. And while he was there, this guy called. Turns out it was her ex-boyfriend who was very upset about being an ex. In fact the phone call sounded so familiar to Nate that he realized that once he *was* that guy. He had called his ex-girlfriend and she had had some guy over. And he remembered being upset about it.

A week or two after his one night stand, he went into a bar and saw the bartender run off with some other guy and he felt nothing. Why? Because he didn't care. Which would you rather be? The guy crying on a payphone in the rain or the guy sitting at a bar with a beer? This is the power of not caring.

How To Not Care

Not caring isn't easy. It's something most people have to learn. We are all taught from a very early age that people who don't care are wrong and evil. We are supposed to care about our parents, our girlfriends, out boyfriends, our children, our friends, our careers, and countless other things. In fact, we are even supposed to have a list of things we care about called 'priorities'. This goes beyond getting rid of your fear of guilt. This is true apathy we're going for here.

So how can we stop caring? By figuring out what to care about and what we just shouldn't give a damn about. There's no reason to diversify your caring into all these different things. Pick something you care about and take that one thing and make it more important than everything else. Don't make it the top priority on your list. Make it the *only* thing on your list. It's important that you make this thing something that's not likely to run off on you. Something like your car. Or maybe your career. Or maybe yourself. Whatever it is, it shouldn't be somebody else because if all you care about is one other person it's likely to make you do some stupid things when that person betrays you. That's not to say that everyone will betray you but it's an unnecessary risk.

By only caring about one thing you make it possible for you to not care about everything else. For example, if you decide that the thing you care about is your career, then you can stop worrying about if your lover is cheating on you or if maybe you have a drinking problem or if anyone else in your life is happy or even likes you at all. See, all of a sudden, you don't have a bunch of problems. You have one problem. Just like that.

The Power of "So What"

Once you learn to not care, you'll be amazed how simple life will become. A school bus goes off a cliff. A plague kills a bunch of people in Zaire. Terrorists blow up a day care center. Your dad has cancer. Who cares? Not you! Plenty of people have lots of problems because they care so much but not you.

Sure, there are those who will say you are 'insensitive' or 'selfish', but these are just people who want you to care about what they care about. There's no need for that. Just say, "So what." and move on.

People who care about things are people who get things like heart attacks and migraines. The stress of caring about things kills people. Not caring doesn't just make life easier. It's actually healthy. It's hard to ruin your life when you're dead, so you should get your health perks where you can.

I realize this chapter is kind of short, but guess what? I don't care.

Chapter 13

Have A Party

Congratulations. This is the last chapter in Part One. From here on out we start getting into some serious ways to Ruin Your Life. So before we get there it's important that you know how to have a party. See the thing about throwing a party is that you get to deal with the aftermath of the party. You will ultimately be blamed for the party's success or failure. And if the cops show up, it's you who has to deal with them. Luckily we've already covered that.

Types of Parties

The first thing you need to figure out is what kind of party you want to have. Since the preparations for different kinds of parties vary wildly, I'll have a section for each type. There are basically five types of parties: Formal, Casual, Close Friends, Hot Tub, and End of the World. Knowing which type of party it is before people start showing up will help avoid potentially awkward situations. There's nothing like having your girlfriend show up in a thousand dollar dress only to have some guy spill Budweiser on it.

The Formal Party

We'll start off with the party you'll least likely want to host. A good formal party takes a lot of planning and a lot of money. While formal parties can be a lot of fun, they can also be a lot more trouble than they're worth. Still, the ability to throw a good formal party can be a valuable asset so here are a few pointers.

Guests

You should invite only people who know how to behave themselves for this party. You don't want to spend a bunch of time and money only to be embarrassed by a good friend with bad manners. A party like this is for close, well-behaved friends, relatives you don't hate, and acquaintances you want to know better.

Invitations

The invitations should be professionally made unless you have a really nice printer. They should set the tone for the sort of party you want it to be. Make sure you have the addresses for all of your guests. Don't hand deliver these. And make it clear that people need to call and RSVP, but assume that at least an additional 20% will come without doing so.

Place

Unless you have an extremely nice house, you should rent a place. Preferably, you should rent a place that has its own staff so you don't have to hire a bartender. No one should be pouring their own drinks at this thing and you don't want to have to do the honors yourself.

If you live near the water, you should try to find a waterfront place. Just the view of the water makes an okay place seem amazing. Whatever you do, try to choose a place that appears impressive. You want your guests to be excited when they first see the place so don't rent out the local Mason Hall unless it's a hell of a building.

Clothing

If you're hosting a formal party you're going to want to look better than everyone else there. If you don't have something really nice, rent something. You want to match the style of the party. At the same time, if you're the sort that would never be caught dead in a tux, don't get one. Instead go to an upscale clothing store and find a set of clothes that are your style but cost like twice as much you'd normally spend. Expensive clothes may seem like rip offs, but they tend to be worth every penny. And don't forget to get some good shoes if you don't have some already. While you're out and about, you may as well get a good haircut and a shave too. You'll never be able to shave as close as a traditional barber can. I know all this may seem a bit excessive but that's the idea with a formal party.

Food

Hopefully the place you rented will provide food, if not just remember that people are going to be dressed in expensive clothing and drinking so try not to make the food too messy. Also try to make the food easy to carry around unless you're having a dinner party. Be creative here. Better yet find someone who knows what they're doing to be creative. Bad food can wreck a formal party so be sure to try out everything beforehand.

Drink

Again hopefully whatever place you've rented out has a cash bar. If not, then hire a bartender, a real bartender. Not just some friend of yours that can make a rum and Coke. If you have to provide the alcohol for this party, buy mid-shelf stuff except for a bottle or two of top shelf scotch.

Do NOT get a keg. Kegs are rarely a hit at formal parties. I had an attorney friend who bought a keg of Belgian White for his party and if it weren't for me that keg would have still been full at the end of the night. He was practically begging people to drink beer that would cost $5.00 a pint in most bars.

Other Notes

Ultimately, if you ask me, formal parties are better to attend than to host. On the upside cops are rarely if ever a problem at parties like this and a well put together formal party will stick in a friend's mind better than most parties. Besides, if you're going to ruin your life you might as well do it in style.

The Casual Party

The problem with formal parties is that there are expectations on all sides. People expect everything to be nice and people feel like they need to be as impressive as their surroundings. This is why the most common sort of party you should have is the casual party.

Invitations

You don't need printed invitations, but if you choose to have them, deliver them in person or on Facebook. There's no need to spend postage. They should not be fancy or on really nice paper. What you'll likely want to do is just call up your friends and tell them to call their friends. Tell them they can bring stuff if they want but don't make it a requirement. If there happens to be anyone in particular you don't want there, make sure you make that clear. Another thing you'll want to get across is whether or not you're going to allow drugs. You don't want someone lighting up a joint in front of your cop friend after all. And on the flipside, you don't want your friend with the really good pot to leave his stash at home.

Place

It's a casual party and you're throwing it so unless there's a good reason to do otherwise, the party should be at your place. This of course means that you're going to have to clean. This does not mean toss everything into one room. You never know when some drunk guy will barge into an off-limits room while looking for the bathroom. You're trying to create an atmosphere here so don't spoil the illusion.

Clothing

The best thing about casual parties is you can wear whatever the hell you want. In fact it's best that you wear nothing flashy unless that's how you normally dress. Just make sure your clothes are clean and you'll be just fine.

Food

No one is expecting anything amazing here. Pizza is always a good bet. Get three types: supreme, pepperoni, and veggie. This way you've covered all your bases just in case your buddy brings his vegetarian girlfriend. It's also a good idea to have a bowl or two of chips just in case the pizza guy is late.

Drink

Yes, nothing quite goes so well with pizza than an ice-cold beer. But not everyone drinks beer. Be sure to have at least some mid-shelf rum and/or vodka along with some mixer. Refer to chapter two for advice on beer but if someone shows up with any malt liquor or wine coolers make them drink only that.

Other Notes

Odds are you're not going to run into too many problems with a casual party. In fact there's hardly any difference between a casual party and just a good Friday night. On the other hand if all you ever throw are casual parties, you'll never be known as the party guy.

The Close Friends Party

The problem with casual parties is that you never really know when someone you don't want to be there is going to show up. Word gets around that there's a party and the next thing you know your girlfriend's ex-boyfriend is drinking your beer. This is why sometimes it's better to have a small party with a few close friends.

Invitations

You should invite people personally and when you do be sure to explain that this is a small party. You should let them know that you're just having a party for your good friends. You should also try to invite people that get along and fit together fairly well. This is not a party to meet new people. This is a party for the Crew.

Place

You almost have no choice but to have the party at your place. You're doing the party equivalent of Springsteen playing a small club in Jersey. It's small, it's intimate, and it should be fucking awesome.

Clothing

These are your friends. It's your place. Wear whatever the fuck you want.

Food

Chips are good. Pizza is good, but don't get something from Pizza Shack. Your friends deserve better than that. Get the pizza from the best place in town. It'll probably be some non-franchise bar. Or if you happen to have a grill, make it a BBQ and get some good meat. Don't want pizza and BBQ? Get some food from a good Chinese place. The nice part about small parties is you can spend a little extra on things like food and drink.

Drink

If you even think of having Monarch or Budweiser at this party, you're not a good friend. You are ruining your life and these are the people who've stuck with you. Don't insult them by giving them cheap alcohol. Everything here should be top shelf, with the exception of the rum. Top shelf rum isn't for mixing so it's best to just go for mid-shelf on that.

Buy a bottle of single-malt 12-year-old Scotch. Not everyone is a Scotch drinker but everyone respects Scotch.

Other Notes

In a way the Close Friends Party is like a bottle of Scotch. It's not for crazy epic nights of debauchery. It's for celebrating the life you're living. The idea here is to take time out from all the shit in all of your lives and just have a good time. Close Friends Parties should be thrown once or twice a year and never more than four times a year.

The Hot Tub Party

Close Friend Parties are great but let's face it, sometimes you just want to see a stranger drunk and naked. And if you don't, then you're reading the wrong book. The problem with nudist parties is that the people heavily into nudism are people you never want to see naked. Rather than having a party full of nudists, you should simply come up with an excuse for people to take off their clothes. This is what hot tub parties were made for.

Invitations

No invitations. You invite people by telling everyone you know that you're having a party and there is a hot tub involved. You tell them to tell their friends and their friends' girlfriends. You should also mention that swimsuits are NOT required. At the same time make sure that you make it clear that it's not just a hot tub party. The reason for this is that there are plenty of people who will say they are not hot tub people but when their three best friends hop in, they change their minds. Let them know a hot tub will be there but getting in the hot tub is not required.

Place

Well, obviously you need a place with a hot tub. If you don't have a hot tub, find someone who does. Tell them that you'll pay for everything and even help clean up. Bribe them. Explain to them that having a hot tub and not having a hot tub party is a crime and that you've already invited everyone anyway so there's no use in fighting it.

Clothes

Here's the thing. You're going to lose your clothes. And I don't just mean, take them off at the party. I mean they will likely be lost. Don't wear anything you really care about. Instead wear clothing that is easily replaceable and have nothing in your pockets that you want to keep. Also be sure to have some towels, but not too many. Have like four towels. That is enough so that it won't appear like you're trying to get people to run around wet and naked.

Food

You don't need anything too fancy for a party like this. In fact, at a party like this, food is optional. But whatever you might bring make sure it's cheap and there's a lot of it.

Drink

Do NOT buy top shelf stuff for this party. Still try to be respectable though. A bottle of mid-shelf rum and vodka and two cases of good but not great beer should do it. If you feel like spending a little extra, get a keg, but make sure you have other beer as well for when the keg runs out.

Other Notes

One of the most important things about a hot tub party is that you not be afraid to get naked. You don't have to have the greatest body. Odds are none of them do either and even if they do they probably don't think they do. It's okay if you're the first one to toss off your clothes and get in the hot tub. The thing to do is grab a bottle of rum, hop in, and let everyone know that the two rules are no clothes and everyone has to have a drink from the bottle.

The End of the World Party

Admit it. You skipped right to this section and didn't even read the others didn't you? That's fine, but before you even consider having an End of the World Party, you need to reread the chapter on talking to cops and maybe even the chapter on getting arrested because the police will show up to this party. I almost guarantee it.

On the flipside so will everyone else. This isn't called The End of the World Party for nothing. This will be an epic party. A party people tell their friends about for years to come. The kind of party that people are angry they missed.

Invitations

There are no invitations. Instead there are flyers. There are rumors. There are postings on the Facebook and Twitter and Tumblr. Make sure you put flyers around the local colleges. You are inviting everyone who is literate. This is the big one. Any special things or guests you'll have at the party should be listed. And list a starting time of six or seven pm. You want to have a lot of time for this one. People are going to arrive, have fun, go home, call their friends, and come back for more.

Place

You need a house for this party. Preferably a multi-story house. It's also a good idea for the house to be easy to find and if it's not, be sure to have directions on the flyers. A place with more than one bathroom is a must. Also make sure you're aware of all of the exits and I don't mean just the doors. I mean any way you can get in or out of the building. It may become important later on.

If you have anything valuable that you absolutely don't want stolen or destroyed, I highly recommend you put it in any room that has a lock or put it in your car. Any house full of drunken partygoers is going to suffer its share of damage. The trick is to make the party worth it.

You should make the master bedroom off limits to anyone who isn't having sex with you. Now at a party like this having a room off limits is almost impossible so if you happen to see a couple people sneak off to your bedroom, do what I did once: wait a few minutes and then burst through the door, turn on the light, and say in the friendliest tone possible, "Hello, I'm the host of the party and this is my bedroom so unless one of you is fucking me, get out."

Clothes

Wear something comfortable but stylish. You're probably going to end up spilling or having things spilled on your clothes so it had better be something that doesn't stain easily. Have nothing in your pockets. If you have steel toe boots and they don't look too strange with what you have on, wear them. They will help you avoid getting your foot stepped on and if things get out of hand there's nothing to keep someone in line like a kick in the crotch from a steel toe boot.

Food

Fuck food. You couldn't feed all of these people without a goddamn soup kitchen.

Drink
At least one keg of beer, two or three cases of shitty beer, and as many bottles of hard alcohol as you can afford. Also do NOT forget the mixer! The thing that runs out at these parties is mixer. Buy a lot of orange juice, Coke, and Sprite. Buy at least twice as much mixer as you do hard alcohol. And don't forget to buy a shitload of plastic cups. And ice! Get a big goddamn bucket full of ice. You can never have too much ice.

Other Notes
Odds are whether you do them or not, there will be drugs at this party. When you invite half the town to a party it's inevitable. You should not even attempt to stop this behavior. Instead just try to steer it away from public view. Actually you should at no time during this party try to tell anyone else what to do. The idea is for this party to get out of control. It's a good idea to have a loud stereo going constantly because this will make everyone yell which will add to the noise level. This is something you actually want. The noise advertises the party. You walk up to a house with a lot of noise and you know things are probably going to get a bit crazy.

When the cops arrive it's important that you not try to hide the fact that there's a party. They wouldn't be there unless somebody called. Answer the door politely and tell them that this is a party for your buddy who joined the military and is shipping out tomorrow. A lot of cops are ex-military and can respect a cause like that. Apologize for the noise and if they have any specific complaints let them know that the culprits have already been thrown out for their behavior. And before they leave, thank them and tell them you appreciate their concern.

You can only have one End of the World Party a year. Preferably it should be on the same day every year. This way people can look forward to it. It can be your birthday or the Fourth of July or any other damn day. The important part here is to create a local tradition.

Other Parties
Of course there are other parties besides these five types mentioned here but really if you can learn to throw even two of these types of parties and do it well, you'll find your scope of friends will explode. People love someone who throws a good party. And now with all the things you've

learned in part one, you're ready to get serious. You are ready aren't you? Then turn the page and begin THE DESCENT.

Part 2

The Descent

The first part of this book is essentially skills that will make ruining your life both easier and more fun. These are ideas that can be used during the course of ruining your life. Part two is going to get darker and dirtier. These aren't so much skills as adventures. Where part one was mostly about your mindset and social skills needed for that mindset, part two is going to be about things you can do using that mindset.

I'd like to take this opportunity to remind you that anything I might tell you to do is not a command. It's not a recommendation. I'm outright telling you that doing these things will ruin your life. If you do not want to ruin your life, thanks for buying the book and enjoy the read. If on the other hand, you are tired of living your 9 to 5, can't miss my favorite show, hum drum life read on. I am giving you all the tools you need to hit bottom at maximum velocity.

Some of the things I'll be talking about in this section are wrong. Some are illegal. All have a certain degree of fun and done right, all of them work for the story. And we know what that means.

Turn the page and begin The Descent.

Chapter 14

Get High

Yeah, I know that I told you at the beginning of this book that getting into hard drugs is a bad idea. But really, what is this book about other than bad ideas?

I remember back when I was in school they had that classic commercial: An Egg "This is your brain." A cracked egg in a frying pan. "This is your brain on drugs. Any questions?" Yes. Why was that commercial usually followed by an ad for Budweiser? The truth is that drugs, like guns, cars, and political campaigns are exactly as bad as the people using them. Drugs don't kill people. Too many drugs at once kill people.

Drugs Are Bad, M'kay?

Drugs are Nintendo for the brain. They create a new reality within your head, if only briefly. A chance to relax, kick back, and feel high. The people who are against this idea usually fall into two categories: people who have never done drugs and people who quit after doing too many drugs.

The people who have never done drugs are hard to reach. It'd be like trying to explain snow to a guy who has lived his whole life in an African desert. There's no point of reference. This is why most drug movies fail to really show you anything that comes close to what drugs are like. They aren't just a physical experience. They're psychological. And while people who have never done drugs can spout off endless statistics and factoids, they neglect to mention that almost all of these studies are talking about hardcore addicts not recreational users. Just like alcoholics are not your average alcohol drinkers.

Speaking of alcoholics, drug addicts are much the same. The reason for this is that alcohol, despite what commercials might have you believe, is a drug. The problem with addicts is that they can't control their intake of their drug of choice. They want as much as they can get as soon as they can get it. And why not? It's hard to believe there is such a thing as too much of a good thing. But a lot of ex-addicts tend to treat anyone who does their drug of choice as an addict. Here's the thing, if you know what your own limits of self-control are, then good, do what you want, when you want to. If you don't, then you shouldn't be doing any drugs at all until you know yourself at least a little bit better.

However if you're going to do drugs I figure the least I can do is give you a few tips from my days in the drug culture.

Which Drugs?

It's important to decide beforehand which drugs you're going to do and which drugs you're going to avoid. Here are my recommendations. Really you shouldn't take any of my advice here. You should do like Nancy Reagan and Just Say No. But like a father who gives his teenage son a condom, I want you to be prepared for the mistakes you're likely to make.

Marijuana

Pot is one of the easiest and safest drugs to buy and use. In some states, it's even legal. Despite what anyone says, it has no addictive chemicals in it. You can form a pot habit but unlike nicotine or caffeine there's no chemical in it that you become dependent upon. There are those who say it's a 'gateway' drug. This is half true. Doing any street drug opens you up to the concept of doing other street drugs and pot is usually everyone's first drug experience. It's also incredibly difficult to overdose on pot. The nice thing about marijuana is that it's a very relaxing high and getting off of it isn't very difficult.

LSD

Acid is tricky. You want to be in the right mood with the right people in the right place for acid. You want to be nowhere near anything that can easily hurt you. It's a fun drug but not something you want to do too often. It's like bungee jumping. Anyone who does it too much is kind of a freak. Ultimately it's something you should probably try once just to see things from a new perspective. As with all drugs, you should only get acid from someone you trust.

Cocaine

Plan on having a long night? Need more energy than a Red Bull can give you? Want to feel really good for a short while? If you said yes to any of these questions, then cocaine is the drug for you. Don't even think about doing crack. There's no real reason too. Cocaine will work just fine. A little snort and you'll be ready for an 18-hour night. Cocaine is addictive however and a little goes a long way. Also people who do a lot of cocaine tend to be really fucking crazy. The human body is not meant to be up for six days straight and when it does, it gets some really nutty thoughts. So it's best to save this for special occasions and really try to find a connection who likes selling it more than doing it.

Heroin

Heroin is a girl who wants to have sex all the time and when you don't want to, she stabs you with a fork while you're sleeping. The high is among the best you'll ever find, unfortunately the low is far lower than you can imagine. Getting off of heroin is like jumping out of a car at 80mph. It is so painful that you'd rather just get another fix than eat or sleep or work or do anything worth doing. It is the sort of all-consuming drug that makes all other parts of your life useless. No one does heroin recreationally.

Meth

Are you fucking kidding me? Did Breaking Bad teach you nothing? You do not want to do meth. The high isn't that great. You get addicted fast. And it's not an addiction you can hide. Tweakers are as bad as heroin junkies. You will lose everything and everyone in your life and not in any way that works for the story. This is a drug that only the dumbest of the dumb fuck around with. Every other drug I've ever encountered, I've met a user who said the drug was great, but that's not happened once with meth users. And most importantly there are better and cheaper drugs out there.

Ecstasy

Ah, ecstasy is one of the more fun drugs out there. The difficulty is getting real ecstasy and not some shit laced with god knows what. Ecstasy makes you feel like you're having the best day of your life regardless of what is going on. And you're going to want to talk. Talk to everyone about everything. And everything you say and hear will be interesting and fascinating…at least to you. It's a good party drug. Bring some water. You'll need it since ecstasy can raise your temperature a bit. This is a drug that fucks with your brain a bit so you don't want to do it too often. There's a reason people call those who do, 'e-tards'.

Pills

There are all sorts of pills but the most common are painkillers like Vicodin or Percocet. These don't really get you too high. They just make it so you don't care about whatever bad thing is happening. And ultimately they're really kind of fun. They do however tend to be more addictive than they are fun so I'm not a big fan. I like something that I want, not something I'll feel I need.

Now that you have an overview of what sort of drugs are out there, let's talk about buying drugs.

Buy Drugs

Buying drugs is like public sex; depending on who it's with and where you are, it can be very, very dangerous. People are killed on a daily basis during drug deals. But remember for the most part all drug dealers want to do is sell drugs.

Most drugs are fairly easy to find in most cities. Start by asking friends. You want to try as many people as you can trust as possible before you start asking strangers.

If you end up getting your stuff from a stranger be sure to buy a small amount. There's no reason to buy $500 worth of product when you don't even know if it's going to be any good. Not to mention you don't want some stranger to know you have $500 in cash in your pocket. And of course there's the off chance he's a cop. If you're not sure about the guy, say you want to sample the goods with him. Most of the time cops won't do drugs with you. Also only buy the amount you originally wanted. Don't let them talk you into a bigger package. When a cop is doing a bust they have minimums they're supposed to bust you for. If someone's trying to talk you into buying more than you want, they're either trying to run a hustle on you or they are cops.

Either way you don't want to do it. Honestly though, there are a lot more dealers than there are cops so the odds are in your favor. Any drug deal should be discreet and fast in that order. You want a minimum of witnesses and no trouble. Don't argue. Don't haggle. Get it done and go.

Do Drugs

While there are plenty of people whose first drug experience is smoking a bong in a room full of people at a party, it's best to do most drugs in private with few people. Don't attempt to nonchalantly snort a little something in the bar. Do it before you go out.

You shouldn't do any drugs that come from any source you don't trust. The one and only time I did heroin I didn't mean to. It was laced in the pot a former acquaintance had. You only want to do the drugs you know you're doing.

It's a good idea to have an anchor when doing drugs. An anchor is someone who either is not doing the drugs you're doing or is significantly less high than you. This is the person who will at least attempt to keep you out of trouble. You should be sure to make your anchor aware of what drugs you are on. This is both to prepare your anchor and so if you happen to take too much and overdose he can tell the docs what you're on. That brings me to another point; DON'T overdose! It's easy enough to figure out what your limit is. Don't go beyond it. It's hard to keep a drug habit quiet if you're at the hospital.

Quit Drugs

Eventually if you have a brain in your head you'll stop doing drugs, hopefully not due to legal or health troubles. The best way to stop doing drugs is the same way you started; slowly. Cut down from every day to every other day, then twice a week, then once a week, then twice a month, and so on. This makes it not only easier to do but helps cut down on the withdrawal.

Now do keep in mind some drugs have withdrawals that can't be avoided or lessened. Withdrawal is the price you pay for the fun you've had. If at all possible, you'll want to get yourself out of the city and away from where it's even possible to get drugs. Or failing that, surround yourself with people who hate drugs and will help you.

Drugs can be a lot of fun. They can create situations and ideas and feelings you'd never have otherwise. But they're not something you ever want to have to depend on. Like your days of drinking wine coolers, it's not something you want to do forever.

Chapter 15

Be Unfaithful

The Case For Cheating

The first time I was married, my wife worked in a bar. From time to time, I would hang out there for a couple hours waiting for her to finish her shift. Actually it was just a good excuse to hang out in a bar and when I say 'from time to time', I mean every night. Anyway, being a fidgety person, I would often fiddle around with my wedding ring. So one evening I'm sitting at the bar casually flirting with the cute bartender while playing with my wedding ring. I order a Black Russian and when it arrives, I absent-mindedly put my ring on the bar. Not ten seconds later, a dead ringer for a girl I had a crush on in high school comes up and says, "Going through a divorce?" I bite my tongue. I keep thinking, "My wife is getting off very soon and everyone here knows her. There's no way to pull this off. Shit." I finally say, "No....damn it." And she half smiles, says, "Too bad." And wanders right out of my life.

The point of this is that I remember that moment and I hate it. I wanted to say, "Yes! She left me this morning for a coworker of hers and never wants to see me again. I'm devastated. Can we go somewhere else and talk about it?" I regret not taking the chance. In fact I regret that more than I have ever regretted the handful of times I've cheated on anyone else. (This may have something to do with the fact that a month later she left me for one of her coworkers.)

You want to ruin your life and have a good time doing it? Be unfaithful. Not only is it fun, but it will totally screw with the status quo of your primary relationship. And believe it or not, that's a good thing.

When it all comes out, you'll be forgiven or you'll be free. Either is better than the steady doldrums that most established relationships fall into sooner or later. Best of all, you'll never have to spend the rest of your life wondering 'what if…'. Relationships end and you're going to really hate yourself when you remember staying faithful to the person who took your car, burned down your apartment, and slept with your father. Consider it a pre-emptive strike.

Slavery is Outlawed, Unless You Call It 'Marriage'

Look, there are couples that are married for fifty years and stay faithful to each other. But do you really want to be like them? Whenever you see these couples, there's always one person who talks up a storm about their perfect marriage and the other one who looks like a prisoner of war who doesn't dare utter a sound without the chatterbox's permission.

Sure, no one will say this is the right thing in public. But millions of people have done it, are doing it, and plan to do it some more. This is why Clinton's approval ratings actually went up after the intern scandal. This is why Robert James Waller can write The Bridges of Madison County, a trite little crappy book about a woman cheating on her husband and getting away with it without regret and have it turn into one of the best-selling books of all time. The concept of being with one person for the rest of your life became stupid around the time humans started living past the age of thirty. It would be like someone saying you could only drink rum for the rest of your life. What if you want vodka one day? This doesn't mean you love rum any less. You just want a little vodka. (Or perhaps you want to live dangerously and have both. Mixed drinks are good after all.)

Can You Keep A Secret?

The problem with cheating on someone is that you now have a secret and very few secrets stay secrets forever. Cheating leaves evidence. (A receipt, a picture, a baby.) Things happen that you can't possibly control. Eventually you're going to be found out. The key here is not to keep the secret forever but to let it out at the right time. Prepare for it. Be ready to move out if you think it'll come to that. Wait until it seems like things are going really well or maybe you just bought tickets for a vacation with your significant other. It's best to make sure that when it's time for confession that they have as much to lose as possible while you're entirely prepared for whatever might happen.

The Aftermath

No matter what, this will not end pretty. There are no storybook endings. Even in the unlikely event that you run off together with your mistress, how could you ever trust each other not to cheat again with someone else? And if you just break up or worse, are caught, that's not going to be nice either. But this book is about ruining your life, what did you expect? The hammer will fall one day. And when it does, you had best be prepared.

So, here's how you handle it: Tell the truth. I realize this sounds beyond stupid, but trust me on this one. You see, you're expected to lie. Everybody lies about being unfaithful. That is why the best defense is no defense at all. It's hard to fight someone who won't fight back. Let them scream and yell. Let them throw your stuff out on the lawn. The crazier they act, the calmer you respond. You will appear to be the sane one, seeking only understanding. Don't even ask for forgiveness. It's funny how people are reluctant to condemn someone who is already condemning himself. (Note: This does not work in a court of law.)

Of course a lot of this is an act. It isn't like you actually regret what you did. And why should you? Regretting it isn't going to make it magically go away. Just think of it as a learning experience. Just be happy that you have the ability to cheat. There are a lot of people who don't even have anyone to cheat on. They just have some lotion and an internet connection. At least you're not one of those people, right? Right??

Remember cheating on someone is like buying drugs. It can be fun, but there are people out there who just want to hurt you and take your money. So as I told a slutty ex-girlfriend of mine, "Remember who you're fucking with." Which of course leads to the next chapter…

Chapter 16

Get A Fuck Buddy

Sex is one of the things in this world that drives everyone nuts sooner or later. If you're having a lot of sex with someone, odds are you'll go along with whatever crazy ass idea they might have, like getting married. But maybe you've already been married. Or maybe you just know better. Whatever the case, what you really need isn't another relationship. What you need is a fuck buddy.

Fuck buddies are just like girlfriends only you don't have to buy them dinner or worry about hurting their feelings. Believe it or not, there's a lot of people out there who just want to get laid. And I'm not just talking about guys. Most the women I've met have had one or more fuck buddies. They're low maintenance and get the job done and won't bitch about you taking off for a week or two with no explanation. Ultimately a good fuck buddy is like a living sex toy.

Finding a Fuck Buddy

A more politically correct term for fuck buddy is a 'friend with benefits'. This term is used by people who want to get off but want to pretend that they aren't just using someone for sex. I think fuck buddy is more accurate. Anyway, many times you already know a potential fuck buddy. They're that friend who you never went out with because they have some sort of problem. They're too sensitive, they're into drugs, or maybe they don't have a job. Whatever the case, they just didn't have that thing you were looking for. Until now. See, the number one quality you're looking for in a fuck buddy is some sort of deal breaking thing that makes you sure you'll never ever want a real romantic relationship with them. This is important. You cannot fall for your fuck buddy. It's against the rules. So it's better to stack the deck by knowing from the outset that there's something about your fuck buddy that makes them strictly temporary.

This brings up another point. You don't want to keep any one fuck buddy for too long or through no fault of their own, they'll become attached. This becomes a problem when you find someone you actually want a relationship with. So it's best not to have a fuck buddy for more than a few months. It's okay to go back to previous fuck buddies after a year or two, but you do need to space it out a bit to make sure they understand you're not interested in anything more than sex with them.

Ground Rules

Unlike romantic relationships where keeping things undefined can be a great strategic tool, in a fuck buddy situation, you want to make sure that everyone is always on the same page. So here are a few rules that should be suggested immediately.

1. No Spending The Night

Yes, it's nice to have someone sleeping next to you at night, but a fuck buddy is there for sex. That's it. Spending the night implies intimacy that shouldn't be there. Remember, you're fucking not making love.

2. No PDAs

Public displays of affection let the world know someone loves you and that you are spoken for. Neither of these things should be true in a fuck buddy situation. And the real danger is that you'll not only confuse other people, but you may get confused yourself. If a fuck buddy is going to become a significant other, then it's after that conversation that PDAs are okay.

3. No Questions

You don't want to know who your fuck buddy is dating or even if they are dating. And they don't need to know anything about your relationships. This is sex for sex.

4. No Presents

If you happen to go to dinner with your fuck buddy, you each pay. You don't buy gifts and you don't accept gifts. This is not a relationship.

There are other rules of course but they generally have to do with a particular situation. Such as if it's a coworker, they can't say anything about it at work. Or if they have a history of stalking that they always have to host the sex. The key thing here is you want to make sure it's clear that you're not in a relationship and anything is okay outside of your fuck buddy arrangement.

Full Disclosure

Under no circumstances should you feel obligated to talk about your life with your fuck buddy. Share whatever you want, but keep in mind that a fuck buddy is not someone to share a secret with. On the other hand if you do have a significant other or start seriously dating someone, you'll want to divulge the existence of any fuck buddies. Best to get those things out of the way quickly. Don't worry. People are more understanding of this than you'd think.

Ruining your life right is a careful process. The whole idea of this book is to make ruining your life a controlled burn and that means that you want to share information whenever it might get out just to avoid information getting out of your control. Remember fuck buddies should be discreet, not covert.

A good fuck buddy is someone who gets you off and goes away when you ask them to. And just like sex toys, if you have too many of them, some people might start to think you're weird. Not that that's necessarily a bad thing.

Chapter 17

Quit Your Job

Unless you are one lucky bastard like my friend Jason who works at Pixar, you probably don't like your job. In fact it's probably the sort of thing that you think to yourself you'll quit one day when you find something better or win the lottery or marry up. Well this chapter is all about making that one day TODAY.

Yes, as you read this, you may be thinking "Yes, but Jack I need my job. It makes me money to pay my bills and buy Adam Sandler DVDs." I understand. But hear me out. For starters, this book is not called "Make Your Life Really Comfortable and Nice". It's called "Ruin Your Life". Quitting your job will most definitely make things like bills and seeing Adam Sandler on your television more difficult, but that's just the down side.

There are many good things about quitting your job.

Power

As long as you've toiled at your job, you've had that boss who could fire you at a moment's notice for no reason at all. Sure, he might be a nice guy. You might even get along with him. But like Mom and Dad when you were a kid, the boss gets to tell you what to do.

Until now. There is a real power shift the day you quit. All of a sudden your boss is just another person in an office. Some business guy who takes himself too seriously. And you, you my friend, are FREE.

I recently quit a job and at the bar last week I saw one of my former co-workers. He looked at me like a prisoner looking at an escaped convict. As if he wanted to say, "How did you do it?" For many people, a strong thing they call a 'work ethic' stops them from even considering an idea like quitting. We'll talk about that in a moment. The second you realize that you can quit a job any time is the second that you realize you have the keys to your own prison.

Work Ethic

Let's get something straight. A strong work ethic does NOT mean dedication to your job. A strong work ethic means you know when to work and when not to work.

Jobs are like relationships. Often in the beginning they are a lot of fun and then as time goes on, the fun stops. Of course it's hard work, that's why they pay you, but you have to realize when it goes past the point of hard work for hard cash and to the point of indentured servitude. Like any relationship, you need to see when it might be time to move on. And again like a relationship, you should move on not because you found something else, but because you want to move on.

There are jobs I've had for years and jobs I've had for minutes. Once I had a job for five minutes. It was a roofing job. A three-story house with a steep roof. The foreman wanted me to "Sweep all those loose shingles near the edge off so people don't fall." I realized right there and then that this was not a job I wanted so I quit on the spot. This was because of my strong work ethic. I knew that they were not paying me enough to potentially fall off a goddamn house. My work ethic told me that I could get a better job (i.e. a job where falling off the roof is unlikely).

Now What

So you've quit your job. What now? The answer is the best thing of all: ANYTHING. You can do whatever you want. Go back to school. Start a life of crime. Toss paint on a canvas and call yourself an artist. Make a cardboard sign and hang out by freeway off ramps. Join the military and get paid to kill. Follow your childhood dreams of being the best E-Z Bake Chef in the world. Or take my approach and write a book about quitting your job. Once you quit your job, you'll realize that there are thousands of opportunities out there for you.

Remember that scene in Fight Club where Brad Pitt puts a gun to the head of that convenience store guy and makes him go back to school to follow his dream of what he really wanted to do? Why wait for that to happen? Is that what it takes? Someone putting a gun to your head? You're brighter than that, aren't you? Take control of your life. Quit that job you hate and go after what you want. Sure, you might be hard up for cash in the short term, but in the long term, you will be happier. On the other hand, it may ruin your life. Then again, I've ruined my life countless times and I'm happy.

Remember, every day is a day off after you quit.

Chapter 18

Move In With Mom

While ruining your life, it may become necessary to lower expenses. Doing things like quitting your job, getting arrested, and doing drugs tends to deplete your finances fairly quickly. Wouldn't it be easier if you had no rent or mortgage to pay? Wouldn't it be better if someone else paid the bills so you could spend your money on more important things like beer and drugs? Sure, most of your exes won't take you back. But the one girl who will always be there is Mom.

She carried you in her womb for nine months. She raised you into the person you are today. And using some of the techniques found in this book not to mention your lifetime experience of asking mom for things, I'm sure you can find a way to convince her that it's for the best if you move in temporarily while you get back on your feet.

Same As It Ever Was

Living with mom? How lame is that? That's right, as lame as it was back when you were sixteen. Sure it sucks, but look at the advantages. All of a sudden your responsibility level is almost non-existent. You take that extra room that your mom has and make it a base of operations. You didn't spend most of your teenage years at home did you? This isn't the place where shit happens. This is just the place where you keep your shit. Besides, as I've said before, there are advantages to people not knowing where you live.

Mom might be reluctant to take you back, but the truth is that most people fall back into old patterns easier than they create new ones.

Odds are at least some part of her has missed you.

New Rules

The nice thing about moving back in with mom is that you get all the advantages of being a kid again and none of the disadvantages. You want to stay out all night? Fine. You want to go get drunk? Go ahead. And this time you don't have to use any fake I.D. or hang outside the Safeway asking older 'cool guys' to buy you a six pack.

This time it's all you. With all the money you're saving on rent and bills, you should be able to afford to go out almost every night. After a while, you might even forget that you live with mom. Think of it as a cheap storage unit. It's not as if you're required to spend any real time there.

By the way, be sure not to give out your home number. Get a cellphone or something. The last thing you want is to have some girl call your house and get mom. Either she'll think you're married or worse, she'll figure out the truth.

"Let's Go To Your Place."

You're going to want to remember this phrase. It's never impressive to take a girl back to Mom's place. This means you have to become comfortable not having the home bed advantage. Don't worry. All you have to do is say you have a crazy roommate. (Depending on what kind of person your mom is, this might not be all that far from the truth.)

If you end up in a relationship, you may find it harder to hide where you live. This is when you'll want to play up your mother's age. Tell her you moved away from the crazy roommate and that your mother has early-stage Alzheimer's and that you're just living there to help her. This will make you seem like a caring son rather than a just a grown man living with his mom.

Movin' Out…Again

Sooner or later you're going to want to leave mom's house again. Hopefully you've saved some money and the move will go easily. The important thing is to not burn your bridges. Make sure you leave on a good note. Leave the place cleaner than you left. Leave your mom a gift of some sort to thank her for her hospitality. You're going to want to kiss ass a little bit. After all, you never know when you might want to go back home to mom's house again.

Chapter 19

Go Out With Teenagers

Remember high school? Remember how trying to get to first base back then was as much of an achievement as your favorite team making the play offs? Did you ever think, "Y'know, if I only knew then what I know now. If only I could go back…."?

Well, guess what? You can. Sure, back when you were a sophomore, that seventeen-year-old had you wrapped around her little finger. She was a total mystery and you loved nothing more than to play the detective. You were so naïve. But now, you've learned. You've grown. You're a bit brighter, a bit richer, perhaps, even a bit more attractive. And there's probably a high school right near where you live. And those high school students still look as good as they did back then. Only nowadays they wear less clothing.

Age of Consent

Now, there are some things you should probably be aware of if you're going to go out with a teenager. While there might be a few social obstacles in this endeavor, you probably need to pay more attention to any legal barriers. This is fairly important. After all, it's one thing to go 'all the way', it's quite another to go all the way to prison.

Luckily the Internet can help you out here. Before you go after that young hot thing, make sure she's not too young.

Remember when your high school crush was going out with that fucking college kid or worse, someone old enough to be her parent? Smile because this time, it's your turn.

Parents

Granted, there are a lot of good things about going out with a teenager, but there are also a handful of major obstacles that you had better be prepared for. The biggest ones of course, are the parents. Luckily, parents today are more open-minded than they used to be and many are completely unaware that they even have children. Still, there are others who will take more than a just a passing interest in your interest in their child. This is where your abilities to lie and tell the truth come in. You will want to assure them that you have the utmost respect for their kid. You'll also want to emphasize the emotional bond you share and minimize the physical bond. No parent really wants to know who their kids are having sex with. Therefore it's best to remind them of simple things they can't disprove. Do NOT use the word 'child' or 'children'. Remind them that you both have a common goal: the teenager's happiness.

If it really becomes a major problem it might be good to minimize your contact with the parents. Come to think of it, that's probably a good idea regardless of how much they like you. You may also want to double check those laws to see who has the authority to press charges on you should you do something illegal.

Morals

Now might be a good time for me to explain that I don't really condone taking advantage of people, even in the pursuit of ruining your life. However, there is nothing really morally wrong with going out with a teenager. And when I say going out, I mean having a physical romantic mutual relationship. I'm not talking about situations where adults are pressuring teenagers into having sex. Some teenagers are ready for sex, others are not, be sure you know which sort of teenager you're with. Doing things like getting a teenager drunk and having sex with them can cause enormous legal hassles and given the wrong psychotic parents, possible health issues as well. Not good.

Long Term

Can a relationship with a teenager work? Sure. It's not like they're teenagers forever. Maybe you found your Soulmate and you were just born the wrong decade. Then again, they are teenagers and the years after that mean a lot of different changes, one of those changes might be losing you. But you can look at the bright side: that high school is still there and class sizes are getting bigger and bigger.

Ultimately, going out with a teenager is like riding a crotch rocket motorcycle at 200mph: it's fun, memorable, and dangerous if you don't know what you're doing. Just be ready to slow things down if you need to and don't do it in front of cops.

Chapter 20

Find The Love of Your Life

I know you're probably thinking, "How can finding the love of my life ruin my life?" I mean, being a drunk, dating teenagers, lying, cheating, getting arrested, all obvious great ways to ruin your life, but this? How can it be?

Well let me tell you, out of all the possible ways I've told you to ruin your life, this is the best one yet. Allow me to explain.

Life Is Not A Movie

We've all been raised on television, books, and movies where the boy finds the one girl he's supposed to be with or the girl finally finds her True Love in the friend she's always had. We watch movies like The Princess Bride and When Harry Met Sally and when we meet someone, we try to make our own movie. (Sometimes literally given the right partner.) It's only natural. I think we're all romantics at heart no matter how jaded we become.

The most jaded guy I know happens to be in love right now. It's an amazing thing. He's stopped screwing three different women. He spends hours talking to this one girl on the phone. He fucking smiles! This is because he has met someone who has made him believe that just maybe she is The ONE.

But regardless of how it turns out, they will not live happily ever after. We don't get that option. The credits never roll at the right time for the movie of our lives. If we are very lucky, we get to live happily for a while before it all goes to Hell again or worse, we will live happily for a while and then spend the next twenty years in the same emotional doldrums that kept our parents together.

The ONE

There is something within us that makes us think at some point in our lives that there is one person we are meant to be with. As if we are all broken puzzle pieces looking for that other piece that completes us. The idea of The One is why romance is the biggest fiction section in bookstores. Believing in The One is what makes people kill in domestic situations. It is one of the most dangerous beliefs there is.

Yet it is also one of the most seductive. Who doesn't want to be part of Destiny? Especially if it means good sex.

Believing in The One is like believing in God in a way. There is no real hard evidence. There are only bits of circumstantial evidence from time to time that we can't ignore and feel it must mean something. Also not believing in The One is just as horrible and lonely and sad as not believing in God. It's sad to think that there is no one for you and you'll end up in bed alone just like it's sad to think of dying and lying in a box in the ground for eternity. This is why it's best to just assume that The One and God exist. It's like assuming that your hangover tomorrow won't be that bad; it might not be true but it's certainly nice to think so right now.

Finding The Love Of Your Life

This is easier than you think. Whoever you are with right now or whoever the next person you are going to be with is: this is the Love of Your Life. I know it sounds strange and maybe you don't want to hear it, but look at it this way. If you are not with the Love of Your Life, who are you with? Are you biding your time? Waiting for that one perfect person, who by the way, won't be interested in you because that perfect person probably wouldn't steal you away from whoever you're with? Think about it. All the previous relationships didn't work so this must be IT. And if it isn't, then you should move the fuck on. Life is too short to be with someone who you can't even pretend is the Love of Your Life. You're too good to be with someone just because you're afraid to be alone. Ditch'em.

Now What

Here's where it gets really screwed up. Let's say you find that perfect person or allow that they aren't perfect but are perfect enough. Now What? Are you going to spend the rest of your life with this person? Is that it? Will that work? Will they still be cool to be with when you're 70? Will a bus hit them next week? What do you do when they dump your ass because they find someone with a better car and more money? How's THAT for a love story?

See, the thing about finding the Love of Your Life is that you've just done the one thing that is sure to ruin your life: you've made someone else more important than you. If you're serious about ruining your life that is the best possible thing to do, because that person has thoughts and feelings that you can't control and they are not going to always do what you want them to. Not only that, but if they want to leave you for any reason (like for instance you seem to be taking advice from a book you bought about ruining your life), you can't stop them.

The Love of Your Life is not the Love of The Rest of Your Life unless you're very, very lucky. And when the Love of Your Life is gone, well, as anyone who has been there knows, the guy who said, 'It's better to have loved and lost than never loved at all.' didn't know what the fuck he was talking about. Welcome to Hell, pal. Population: You.

Chapter 21

Be A Stalker

As I mentioned in the previous chapter, falling in love is one sure fire way to ruin your life. Mainly because if you happen to fall for someone who doesn't fall for you, then you have a problem. Finding the Love of Your Life is dangerous stuff. So what do you do when the person you like doesn't like you? You are not the first person to have this problem. In days of old, waiting outside a girl's window in hopes of seeing her was literally the stuff of Romeo & Juliet. It was romantic. However, in this day and age of 9-1-1 and restraining orders, you're not called a romantic. You're a stalker. You shouldn't hide from this label. Embrace it.

Relationships are difficult. You never know when someone is going to betray you or hurt you or have a change of heart. So many things can go wrong. Other people can be so cruel. This is why sometimes it's better to just not involve other people. There's nothing wrong with admiring from afar…or perhaps even from very near.

How NOT To Be A Stalker

First, let's start with things you don't do. You do not want to hurt or kill your target. Doing so not only screws up your stalking, but will likely land you in prison. And even if it doesn't, you'll end up having to find someone else to stalk and you already know how hard it is to find the right person. An effective stalker should be able to stalk without the target ever even knowing. This also means you do not write notes, letters, or messages in newspaper clippings, ink, or blood. You must leave no actual evidence.

This is not only for legal reasons. If you leave evidence or let your target know in any way that you are stalking, they will start being more careful, locking doors and windows, and that sort of thing. There's no reason to make your job any harder than it has to be.

Don't call except from payphones. Caller ID has made the hang up phone calls in the middle of the night not so anonymous. Of course if your target knows you in daily life feel free to call from your own phone. Cellphones come in handy for calls while you're outside.

Do not tell people about your stalking. This is your hobby, your passion, and like a collection of porn, you should keep it hidden from everyone in your life. People often don't understand obsession. Remember, the best way to not get caught is don't tell anybody.

Every Breath You Take

The nice thing about unrequited love is that it's easy. You don't have to worry about how the other person feels or whether their family will like you. You don't even have to spend money going out with them. All you have to be concerned with is how high their fence is and their familiarity with restraining orders or firearms.

Modern technology has made it remarkably easy to be a stalker. There was a time when you'd have to actually break into the person's house or physically follow them around. But now thanks to the Internet, webcams, Global Positioning System devices, and digital cameras, you hardly have to leave your house. Of course using some of this equipment without your target's knowledge might not be legal, so be careful.

One Person's Trash…

Once garbage is put to the curb, it is considered public property. This means whatever someone throws away is potentially yours. And when that comes to stalking, it can be very useful. Want to know what they had for dinner last week? Odds are that pizza box is in the trash. Care to see what grocery store they go to and what they buy? Those receipts usually end up in the can along with everything else. Most people just toss away their cellphone bills even though they list every number they called in the last billing cycle. It's really quite amazing the stuff people toss out. If you want to know someone, going through their trash will help.

It's best to grab someone's trash at night. The less people around, the less likely some nosey neighbor will mention it to your target.

Do it quickly. Pop your trunk, dump it in and go. You'll have time to check out your haul later.

The Best Part About Being A Stalker

You've heard the saying "The fantasy is always better than the reality." Well guess what? With the exceptions of Cuban Cigars, good Scotch, and great sex, it's true. And even if the person you are stalking is capable of great sex, I'd be willing to bet they are not as good as you imagine they are. The imagination is a wonderful thing. And props such as articles of clothing, or the smell of perfume can easily augment it. If you take anything, be sure it is nothing they'll miss. Don't take their favorite scarf. Take something you haven't seen them use in the last month.

Keep in mind that unlike in a relationship, when you are stalking someone, it only ends when you want it to end. It's all up to you. Maybe you'll become bored and need a new target. You don't need to worry about your first target getting jealous. You can keep stalking as many people as you have time for. And even if they lock you up, no one can stop you of thinking of your targets whenever you like.

As for how this ruins your life, well exactly how many stalkers do you know who are perfectly well adjusted and happy?

Chapter 22

Get Fat

Every day you see people jogging their lives away. If you ask them what they're doing, they'll say they're getting 'in shape.' However none of them know what they're getting in shape for. It's not like we all have to run a marathon in order to get to Heaven. The human race isn't an actual race. And you're just as likely to be killed in a car accident if you're an athlete as you are if you're a fat bastard.

Big Time

Let's face it. One of the few pleasures in this life that doesn't require a good pick up line or phenomenal luck is good food. Whether it's chocolate, steak, or pizza, we all have our favorite foods. And odds are there's someone we know telling us those foods are bad for us. They say that we'll live longer if we don't eat so much of it, but who wants to live a long life without pizza?

Eating along with sleeping is one of the things you need to survive. It's something you should be good at. Most importantly, it's something you really should enjoy.

The key to getting fat is the exact opposite of getting thin. Do NOT set goals. Don't plan what you eat. Don't even weigh yourself on a regular basis. Just eat as much as you want of whatever you want and enjoy the fact that gluttony is the tastiest deadly sin.

Diet Shmiet

People will say that good exercise and a good diet will keep you alive another five or ten years, but when you add it all up, you'll find you spent those years exercising and eating food you hate. This is no way to live. And it's not as if all the dieting and exercise in the world was going to turn you into that underwear model in the magazine anyway. If you can't be the best at being thin, why not try being the best at being fat? It's more fun.

Diets are for people who want to be told what to do. I mean what could be more basic than what you put into your body? How old are you anyway? Aren't you old enough to make your own decisions as to what you will and won't eat? And does anyone really want to look like Richard Simmons? Forget diets. Eat what you want and be happy.

Besides, here's a little secret, people LOVE fat people. Think of just about any given TV show and you'll find that the fat guy is one of the most popular characters on the show. You think that Cheers would have been on all those seasons without Norm? Hell no! You want people to like your show? Put a fat guy in it.

Larger Than Life

Marlon Brando, Elvis Presley, Orson Welles, John Belushi, Chris Farley, you. Being a fat guy puts you in a very special league. All of these guys knew a good amount about ruining their lives and getting fat. Remember, only the Good get fat. Yes, you're more likely to die of a massive heart attack or any number of other health issues, but you're also more likely to eat an entire supreme pizza with no help and then dig into the ice cream. Who wouldn't want to be that guy?

And don't worry. There are plenty of people who find fat people attractive. It's just more to love as they say. As with anything, you don't want to get too out of control. Try to avoid the three hundred pound mark at least for a while. (People who need MRIs done have to go to the zoo if they're over three hundred pounds.) There's a difference between getting fat and getting enormous. You'll know that difference if they make you buy two tickets instead of one on an airplane.

All in all getting fat is the sort of thing that some people only dream of. You can make that dream a reality with minimal effort. And best of all when you finally do kick the bucket, it'll be all your wheat grass juice, jog five-mile-a-day friends who have to carry your heavy ass in your coffin. Good thing they're in shape.

Chapter 23

Get In A Fight

Most people avoid conflict. They live their lives below the radar trying not to rock the boat. They get their aggressions out vicariously through movies and video games. You do not want to be one of these people. You want to be someone they make movies *about*. Now given that you're going to live your life like a movie you should keep in mind that any movie worth a damn has a good fight scene.

But getting into a fight isn't just about making a good scene. It's about learning what you'll really fight for and how hard you'll fight for it. This is important. If you don't know what kind of fighter you are, then you don't know what you'll do when the shit really hits the fan. And the thing about the shit hitting the fan is that the fewer unknowns there are, the better you can deal with it. The ability to kick ass and the knowledge of how much ass you can kick is invaluable given the amount of assholes there are on the planet.

Choose Your Opponent

This is probably the most important aspect of getting into a fight. If you choose the wrong person to fight then you're just going to get your ass kicked and that's no fun at all. So first off you should be moderately sure you can beat your opponent before you pick a fight with him. But don't pick some small guy either. You're not a bully. You're a fighter. There's a difference.

Another thing to keep in mind is motivation. You can't fight someone just to fight him…Well, you can, but it's not as good for the story and remember what I said about making things work for the story. So make sure that whoever you fight you have a good reason to fight. Notice I said good reason not just any reason. If a guy cuts you off, that's not a good reason. If a guy screws your wife and wrecks your car, that's a good reason.

You don't really have to go looking for a fight generally. If you apply even half of the things I tell you in this book the odds are pretty good you'll find people to fight fairly quickly.

And if someone picks a fight with you, size him and the situation up. If you think you can beat him, go for it. If you know you can't, run away. You're not going to prove anything to anyone by getting your ass kicked.

Fighting: The Rules

When I was a kid and I got into fights people would say that I broke the rules or cheated just because I kicked the guy in the crotch. But these weren't boxing matches. These were conflicts where someone wanted to hurt me and I stopped that happening by hurting them. The only rule to a fight like this is get hurt as little as possible.

There are people who will say that you shouldn't pull hair, scratch, toss sand, kick in the crotch, and all sorts of other things. But the biggest 'shouldn't' in fighting is you shouldn't lose. Ask yourself this: would you rather be the guy who broke a few unwritten 'rules' or the guy bleeding on the pavement who 'fought fair'? That's what I thought.

Weapons

When I say, get in a fight, I do not mean pull a gun or a knife and off the other guy. That's not a fight. That's murder and you do a lot more time for that than for assault. Of course another thing to keep in mind is that since there aren't any rules to a street fight, you never know when some guy whose ass you're kicking will pull a knife or a gun. So it's a good idea to be prepared for this.

When I say 'be prepared', I do not mean carry your own gun. I mean know what to do. If someone pulls out a knife, you have two choices. You can run, which isn't a bad option, there's no point in dying in a street fight. But sometimes you can't run, so the thing to do is give the knife a target. Let him get you in the hand you use least, at that point you use your other arm and hit him as hard and as fast as humanly possible until he falls down or drops the knife.

A gun is a different story. Running from a guy with a gun is just giving the guy target practice. Remember, run from a knife, and rush a gun. You want to give a guy with a gun no room to fire. If you see him pulling it you should get as close to him as possible and be as violent as possible about it. Anyone pulling out a gun during a fight is ready to kill you and that means you're not just fighting anymore, you're fighting for your life. This changes everything. Get the gun away from the guy by any means possible and knock his ass out.

Consequences

It's important to keep in mind that actions have consequences and kicking someone's ass is rarely the last you hear of them. This means that he might come back sometime with friends to kick your ass or he might come back with some cops or that worst combination of cop friends. Whatever the case, it's probably a good idea to have your lawyer's number on speed dial.

If he's not the sort to go the legal route, it might be a good idea for you to do so. Restraining orders are wonderful things if used correctly. You get a restraining order on the guy and all of a sudden if he even looks at you the wrong way, it's a crime.

It's also a good idea if the guy you fight has no information about you or at the very least some false information. The more of his story that turns out to be bullshit the more the cops or if comes down to it, the jury will stop believing him.

Some people might say why go to all this trouble with fighting. But the fact remains, after a righteous fight, even if you lose, you feel better about yourself. The ability and willingness to fight is something that sets you apart from most people. Remember you're ruining your own life. You don't need anyone else trying to do it for you.

Chapter 24

Be A Sexual Customer Service Rep.

I worked at Amazon.com for two years as a customer service representative. When it comes to customer service, Amazon is considered the best in the business. Along with writing, movies, crime, sex, alcohol, and car accidents, customer service is something I know quite a bit about.

The interesting thing is that you can apply customer service techniques to other parts of your life. Many of the tenets of customer service aren't just good customer service ideas. They're good ideas for your life or more specifically, your sex life. Sure, you're supposed to think of sex as a meaningful connection between two people and it's supposed to be the ultimate expression of your feelings for that person, but this isn't love advice. So listen up.

The basic idea of customer service is to keep the customer happy so they will return. However, isn't that also the basic idea of sex?

You want to keep your partner happy so she will come back and not go somewhere else. Right? Well then it's time to learn some customer service fundamentals.

The Customer Is Always Right

You don't like to go down. You don't like to get tied up. You don't like cuddling before or after. Well guess what, pal? Too bad. This is about one thing, keeping the customer (i.e. your partner) happy in bed. If you want to be any good at all at this you'll learn what they want and do it. Why? Because if you do what they want, they will pay you back by doing what you want.

When it comes to sex, the currency we pay in (when we're not paying in cash) is reciprocity. If your partner is not into reciprocating then they are stealing from you and you should treat them like any other thief. You can't get something for nothing. Men don't buy flowers and dinner just for the hell of it. This is why you must go out of your way to make sure the customer is getting everything they want. It's a buyer's market and if you can't provide them with the service they're looking for, they will find it elsewhere. Remember, you're not the only customer service guy in town.

ABC = Always Be Closing

This is a selling technique and really selling is what customer service is all about. Everything you do and say is getting the customer to go all the way. You don't want to give them time to consider other options. You must have confidence. You're not trying to con them because what you are selling you honestly believe is the best product on the market and if you don't believe that, then start believing it because a lover who doesn't believe in their love making ability is exactly like a salesman who doesn't believe in his product.

You have to make them understand that what you want is best for both of you. You're not just looking for the pay off. You want to make it clear that their decision here will be mutually beneficial. By the way, don't use phrases like 'mutually beneficial'. At least attempt to be smooth. You don't have to convince them it's the only option, just that it's the best option. Common sense will do the rest.

Indirect Customer Service

It's not all about sex. At Amazon, we used to answer questions that we knew would not lead to a sale. But what we also knew is that if we were able to give them something they couldn't get anywhere else, then maybe when it came time for the sale, they would remember us. Customer service is about keeping the customer happy and keeping your name on their lips. There is plenty of competition out there and you need every single edge you can get.

So if they need help moving, go right ahead and offer to help. If they're looking for a good recipe or a good movie to rent, have a few suggestions. Odds are, they'll remember it was your idea and you'll get the credit. It doesn't work 100% of the time, but when it does, you've already built a strong basis of trust with your help. And a partner who trusts you is a partner who is willing to go for the more exotic sales.

Repeat Customer

As anyone in customer service will tell you, it is not about making that one sale. Anyone can do that. What good customer service is all about is developing a lifelong relationship. It is about making sure your customer comes to you for all their needs in the future. Why? Because you are the best. Because you are there for them every time. Because that is how you succeed. That is how you turn a business into an empire. Some people may say this is a cold and calculating way to talk about something as intimate as sex. Some say you should go with how you feel and leave everything to chance. You can do that. You could also do that and try to sell cars, but you're not going to be employee of the month with an attitude like that.

Chapter 25

Have A One Night Stand

Tonight in any given bar, nightclub, or party there are people who didn't know each other a few hours ago who are going to have sex. They are not Soulmates. They are not beginning a new long-term relationship. In fact, more than either would care to admit, they are not even all that attracted to each other. But they do share one thing: the desire to not go home alone tonight.

At closing time the prospect of going back to an empty apartment and an emptier bed can make one's standards and inhibitions plummet. Enter the one night stand. The one night stand is like Taco Bell. We know it's probably not good for us but it'll get us what we want quickly and without too much expense.

Let's Spend the Night Together

I'm not going to tell you how to pick up girls. (There's already a fine book called The Game by Neil Strauss that can tell you all about that.) The person you're looking for is the person who is looking for someone like you. Walk in looking to take someone home, try not to put your standards too high, and you'll find that special person. You were made for each other…for tonight anyway. Just try not to look bad or say anything stupid.

As for places to pick someone up for a one night stand, I suggest somewhere you don't usually go. There's nothing to ruin your favorite bar like a fling that happens to be a regular and wants to sit at your table every time you're there.

You're not looking for the love of your life here. You're looking for Miss Right Now. So it's okay if they have no money or a bad car or just a shitload of issues. Just make sure they aren't attachment issues. You don't want to take someone home and wake up in the morning to someone wanting to introduce you to her parents. This shouldn't be too much of a problem though because the sort of person who would go home with a guy she met in a bar isn't the sort who is looking for her next husband.

"Your Place or....Your Place?"

The problem with hooking up with someone you barely know is quite simply that you barely know them. She could be psychotic. She could be married. She could be married to a psychotic. This is why the last thing you want to do is let her know where you live. Sure, share your body, but don't share your address. Remember, you don't want anyone stalking you.

In other words, you're going to want to spend the night at her place or a hotel. This is not a situation where you need the home bed advantage. This is like a pre-season game. No one knows or cares about the game except the people playing and odds are, they won't care either once it's over. Go for the win but don't do anything that'll injure you during the regular season.

Feel free to try out anything you're not sure about. This is a good way to practice things for when you're with your real partner. Have fun. This is a no-harm, no-foul zone. You can't fuck up a relationship that isn't there.

Another thing to keep in mind is that you're not the bad guy here. There's no reason to feel guilty for what you're doing. One night stands tend to have a lot of warning signs that they are just that. And besides it's not like either of you are going to be around later to find out if you feel bad about it. So enjoy yourself.

Elvis Has Left The Building

As for how to leave, there are a number of strategies. There is the usual disappearing before the other person wakes up. Or you could stay and have breakfast. Personally, I would suggest a combination of the two: Wake up first. Get dressed quietly. Take a walk to the local store. This will give you time to reflect on whether or not the person in that bed is someone you want to have breakfast with. If they are, buy some breakfast stuff and maybe a candle or something, go back, make breakfast and be a really cool one night stand person. If, however, upon thinking about it, you realize that this is not the sort of person you even want to look at in the daylight, grab a coffee and maybe some ibuprofen for that hangover you probably have, and head on home.

And keep in mind that just like Taco Bell, it's okay every now and then, but you don't want to do it every night.

Chapter 26

Put The 'Ex' Back In Sex

We all have people in our lives who know us better than we know ourselves. The sort of person who came into our life and reminded us that we still don't know a damn thing about anything. Like a hurricane, they came in, changed our lives forever, and if we were lucky, we still had our house left when they went away. I am, of course, talking about exes.

These are the people who have seen all your tricks, know your secrets, and know how to make you hot or piss you off. If you are murdered, the cops will talk to these people first. And if they end up dead, you better have a good alibi.

"Exes are exes for a reason."

More than one person has tried to tell me that exes should stay exes. After all, there have to be reasons why you're not together anymore and odds are those reasons still exist. But in my opinion, that's the pessimistic way of looking at things. I mean, there are also reasons why you were together in the first place. And I'm willing to bet it has something to do with really good sex. If it doesn't, then I'm not talking about that ex. I'm talking about the other one. The one you still fantasize about when you're alone. The name you want to call out when you're having sex regardless of who you might be with. That ex.

Granted, the fact that you are split up with your ex does not bode well for the future, but that's long term. You already know this person isn't your partner for life, but she might be for tonight.

Hooking Up

I wish I could have a section here on how to hook up with your ex again, but since relationships and people are so different, I can only give a handful of general guidelines.

First off, if you haven't talked to them in a while, ask them out for a drink. Alcohol is a great social lubricant and can help get past the awkward stages of breaking the ice. Also, most people tend to use alcohol as an excuse to do what they really want to do in the first place. So if your ex is up for something more than drinks, they're more likely to make a move when they can blame it on the alcohol. And more importantly, if they don't make the first move, you can make a move and use that very same excuse. Best of all, if it doesn't work out, they just go back to being your ex.

Next, you want to make sure that the rules are in place. You don't want to have a one-night-stand with your ex only to find out that she thought you were starting up the whole relationship again or vice versa. These rules don't necessarily need to be outright spoken. They can be implied. Or if you're kind of a bastard, told afterwards.

Really, when it comes down to how to hook up with your ex again, the bottom line is you did it before so you can do it again. Remember, it's easier to walk a path when you've walked it before.

Second Time Around

The thing that makes having sex with an ex so much better than having sex with someone new is that you already know this person. It's like visiting a place where you went on vacation again. This time you know all the special places to go and hopefully this will make for a much better trip. This also goes the other way around. She likely knows what you like and what you love.

The other fun thing is that some things have no doubt changed since the last time you two hooked up. You've likely both learned some new things and gotten better at old things. People rarely get worse at sex over time. Unless of course you're seventy, but luckily there are pills for that.

It's Over....Again

Since you two have already broken up at least once, it's a good bet that even if you end up back in a relationship, it will eventually end. But like my friend Nate says, "It's easy to go out with my ex-girlfriend because since we broke up before I know I can handle it again." Breaking up with an ex is just confirmation that it was good you broke up in the first place.

On the upside, odds are you have more than one ex who might be a bit nostalgic. Remember the worst they can say is 'no' (and the best they can say is, "YES! YES! OH GOD YES!")

They say you can't go home again, but I say you can visit. Sex with the ex is like driving at 80mph in the snow: people might get hurt but whatever happens, it'll be unforgettable.

Chapter 27

Get Engaged

You might think that ruining your life is a lot easier if you're single. You'd be wrong. Being in a committed relationship is a surefire way to complicate every aspect of your life. As a single guy, you can meet a reasonably attractive and morally questionable woman in a bar, go back to her place, have sex, and no one but her boyfriend will care. Odds are the only thing that might get ruined is the buttons on your shirt when she rips it off. But take that scenario and add a wife back home wondering where the hell you are and what happened to your shirt and your life just got a hell of a lot more interesting.

But before you can have a wife, you have to have a fiancé. And like buying a new car, there are some things you should try before you buy. You walked on the lot, you found one you like; getting engaged is the test drive before you decide this is the one for you. Given the importance and impact of something like this, I thought it might be a good idea to let you know some things to look for and look out for in that prospective mate. (And girls, you can use this list just as well as guys.)

Have Sex

I know this is a no-brainer, but there are still some traditionalists out there who think waiting until you're married to have sex is a good idea. 'Saving yourself for marriage' is like waiting until you're in combat to fire a gun. It doesn't make the experience better. It makes it a hell of a lot scarier. Sure, you might get along on every other level, but if you both like to be on top, or only one of you likes blindfolds and whips, then you're looking at a compatibility issue that almost ensures adultery, divorce, or both. And we haven't gotten to those chapters yet so let's focus on good sex with just the one person for now.

Speaking of good sex, if this is someone you're going to be with for perhaps the rest of your life, you're going to want to do something. For a lot of guys (and some girls), this will go contrary to how you generally deal with sex: Become their sex slave for a night. If you really want to have great sex, it helps to know what your partner likes and why she likes it. Let her tell you every little thing she wants you to do and why she wants you to do it. The reason for this is simple, the more you can please her, the more she'll want to please you. Which of course is why the next night she gets to be your sex slave. Knowing what gets each other off is more important than knowing what each other likes to eat.

Go On A Long Road Trip

Traveling changes a person's environment and leaves only what they've brought with them and their traveling partners. If you want to get to know her, sit in a car with her for twelve hours. Sure, she may seem great at the bar and at home, but what's she like when you're lost in Omaha and you refuse to get directions? What's she like when the air conditioner breaks and you're driving through the desert? Can she pretend to be really sick when the cop pulls you over for speeding?

Yes, it might seem extreme to be stuck in a car for hours or days on end with the same person, but then again, the same can be said of marriage. A road trip is a metaphor for your whole relationship. There will be good points and bad points and points where you want to quit. If there's going to be any problems you might as well get them out of the way now.

Get Mad at Each Other

People I meet who are engaged or married and say with smiles in their eyes that they've never had a fight crack me up. They're like someone juggling grenades and saying they haven't blown up yet. When people get angry, they can sometimes turn really scary and it's not the sort of unknown you want in a relationship. Not only that but different people push different buttons. Having great chemistry is a good thing but sometimes that chemistry is explosive.

Now when I say get mad at each other, I mean really mad. I mean red in the face, wanting to throw things mad. The test here is to see if either of you can control yourselves and if not, why not. Domestic violence isn't how you want to ruin your life. You want your home to be calm so you can handle the outright chaos you've caused everywhere else.

Don't worry. You probably won't have to stage anything. One or both of you will eventually do something to get each other pissed off. And if not, try coming home at four in the morning with no excuse and wearing someone else's shirt.

Lie Together

The more people telling a lie, the more likely it will be believed. Ask the Bush administration. This is why it's important to know if your partner can lie with you when the situation demands it. You don't want to say you were home with your wife on the night in question only to have her say something like, "Yeah, I think he was here. Maybe."

Not only that but watching your partner lie when you know she's lying helps you see what she does when she lies. This means when she lies to you, you might have a better chance of spotting it. And if you can't spot it, good. A good liar can get you out of situations better than a gun.

Get Drunk

There are many, many people out there who are just fun to be around. They tell jokes, have interesting stories and like to do fun things. They make you happy just by being near them. Then you get them drunk and they turn into evil bastards who want you dead. I know.

I used to be one of those drunks. Before you even think of actually going through with the wedding, get drunk together and find out what sort of drunks you are.

There are many things to watch for here. Is she too flirty with other guys while drunk? Are you too jealous? Are you too flirty with other girls? Do you even like each other when you're drunk? Will you hold her hair back when she's throwing up? Will she offer to drive when she sees you want another one? Will she not be too mad you pissed on her plant? The answers to questions like these are more important than anything you'll get in premarital counseling.

Confess Something

You need to be able to tell your partner absolutely anything and know for a fact that she isn't going to tell her friends or in some cases, turn you in. Something to keep in mind here is that you aren't looking for some gullible dupe that you can easily pull things over on. You want someone who is on your side and forgiving. So the thing to do is tell her the worst thing you've ever done. Something that you feel (or at least can pretend to feel) really bad about. See how she takes it. Wait a while. See if her friends start looking at you the wrong way or if her behavior towards you changes.

You may notice I use the word partner a lot in this. That's because that's what she should be. A partner in crime. Someone who is with you no matter what. If she isn't that, then what's the point of getting married? Why would you even want to come home to someone who wouldn't be there for you no matter what? This person needs to love all of you, not just the good sides, but the dark stuff too. And if you're like me, there's a lot of dark stuff.

Another thing to keep in mind is that you want to know her dark stuff also and it's best to get it out of the way now. You don't want her to confess something on your tenth wedding anniversary. You want to know that stuff now. Remember this is a test drive and if all else fails, you can always take the car back to the lot and look for another one.

Get Married

Getting married is not only a big step, it's a big topic. Assuming you two have passed all of these tests, it's time for that most horrible of rituals, the wedding. See ya on the next page.

Chapter 28

Get Married

Whenever someone tells me they're getting married, I always say, "Good. Everyone should do it at least once." I believe this. Fear of commitment is not a good thing. You don't want to miss out on a Soulmate or more importantly the best sex of your life just because you have commitment issues.

Let's get something straight here. Getting married isn't like getting a tattoo. It's not permanent. It's exactly as permanent as hair-dye. And if that doesn't get rid of your fear, think of it this way: committing to someone is just like apologizing to someone, you don't have to mean it. You just have to sound like you mean it.

The Wedding

Guys, I'm sure you have a vague idea of what kind of wedding you want and whatever that idea is you should just keep it to yourself. Because the truth is while you might have a lot of good ideas for what makes a good wedding your lovely wife-to-be has been planning this event in meticulous detail since she was five.

This is why there are a thousand different wedding dresses to choose from and three tuxes. So here's the thing to do: agree with whatever she wants. Go ahead and raise an objection or two, but ultimately give in.

Girls, no one goes to weddings to see the groom. They go to see the bride and you know it. So make sure you look damn good and your hubby-to-be doesn't look too bad. If this is your first wedding, the odds are pretty good that you can get the parents to throw down some serious scratch for the wedding if only out of fear of not seeing the grandkids if they stiff you. Also with wedding number one you can play the "This is only going to happen once in my life, Daddy." card.

Regardless of what sort of personality you have, I highly suggest a remotely classy wedding. This is to make all the relatives you have at least think that you might have grown up.

However, I want to stress that you should NOT make it a big wedding. No one really likes big weddings. If you're spending enough money on the wedding to buy a new car, you've got some serious issues.

The Reception

Rent a place. Trust me on this. You don't want to have this at anyone's house unless you happen to hate that person. Wedding receptions tend to be events where all the unhappy people get plastered and do stupid things so it's best that the janitorial staff of some Slovenian Hall has to clean up the vomit. Make sure the place has a full bar or at the very least that they allow you to bring beer. It's important that there be alcohol at the reception because otherwise no one will have any fun. There are of course certain traditions: the first dance, the garter, the bouquet, etc. As with all previous things, defer to your wife-to-be on this. You might as well get used to that anyway.

Do not stay until the end of the reception. You don't have to see everyone out and really you should leave right around the time your parents are drunk. The reason for this is that if you stay there all night, odds are all you'll do when you get home is sleep. It's better to go home with a couple drinks and a bit of energy left over. Wedding night sex is something special and guys, you're probably going to want to find a chance to jerk off before the main event just so you'll last longer. If possible, try to convince her to keep the wedding dress on.

Girls, when it comes to wedding night sex, you can use the 'this is my wedding night' excuse to get the guy to do just about anything you want him to do. And if they happen to disagree with this, seriously reconsider the wedding.

I Now Pronounce You…

You're husband and wife now. Prepare for the joys of married bliss, which you'll soon find out isn't so much bliss as much as petrified terror. Okay, that's not necessarily true. If you've chosen well, you now have what you've always wanted: a partner in crime and in the bedroom. This may not seem like a good way to ruin your life, but keep in mind that you've now just tied your future to someone you can't control who may end up being instrumental in utterly destroying your life in a manner no book could fully capture.

Congratulations.

Chapter 29

Have Kids

There are some people who think getting married makes you an adult. But really you're not an adult until there's someone you're not fucking calling you 'Daddy'. Children can be the biggest blessing and curse of your life. Children are like those little monsters in Gremlins; they take whatever is around them and create the worst possible combination. If you have hairspray and a lighter within reach, prepare to see a flamethrower. If you have a porn disc hidden somewhere in the living room, they will inexplicably find a way to play it while relatives are over. And if you are giving them food, they will put it everywhere but their mouth. Despite these things, there are many reasons to have kids. Here are a few of them not covered in most books:

People Will Respect You

Despite the obvious evidence that there are millions of truly shitty parents out there, having children makes people think you have your shit together. This is not a permanent impression, but as long as you appear to be a good parent, people will respect you for that even when they have no reason to respect you for anything else.

Part of this is that if you have a little person looking up to you and you are any sort of human at all, you'll end up behaving better than you would normally. Believe it or not this is a good thing. Ruining your life can be tricky. Keep in mind that you want the stories your kid tells about you to be good ones. Sure, they won't always think of you as a God but if you live right and ruin your life properly you will be a Legend.

It's Your Alibi

Where were you last night? Taking care of the kid. Why didn't you come into work yesterday? Kid was sick. Who broke that antique vase my grandfather left me? The kid did it. Nobody questions you when you say that it's the kid. They see you as someone who is taking responsibility and being a good parent as opposed to being someone intent on ruining his life. Kids are the ultimate excuse.

Not only that, but if you train them right, the kid will lie for you. And who's not going to believe a cute little kid?

You Get To Be The Boss

Parents can abandon you. Wives can leave you. Children are the only people who are legally required to stick around and listen to your shit. (At least every other weekend.) They may not always like you, but until they're teenagers, you're the boss and what you say goes.

Kids are the only people who will listen when your excuse is, "Because I said so."

You Get To Be A Kid Again

A grown man buying video games and action figures is a bit odd. And these are difficult things to explain....unless of course you have a kid. Then you can buy all the kid stuff you want. And when you do, you don't seem like some immature irresponsible geek. You seem like a nice parent.

It's amazing the stuff you can get away with if you have a kid with you. You can watch cartoons, buy teddy bear shaped Popsicles, and a Spongebob Squarepants Kite and no one will think you're weird.

Someone Will Love You

This may sound bad but let's face it, if you use even a fraction of the things in this book, there's a good chance you're going to lose friends and loved ones. Your children are like pets in that they're going to love you no matter what....that is unless you give them reason to hate you. I know this may sound like how it is with everyone else but it isn't. No one feels apathy towards his or her parents. It's either love or hate and the truth is that children are built to love you so as long as you don't beat them, try to control them too much, or disown them, you'll do all right. And when it comes down to it, having that son or daughter there for you when you need them is better than anything in the world.

Ultimately having children is one of the biggest, most important things that will ever happen to you. It's your own piece of immortality. In many ways, children are the reason you're here. And really if by some miracle you're alive when you're eighty, you're going to need someone to pay for the old folks' home. Having kids is like joining the Army; it'll turn you into a new person provided it doesn't kill you.

Chapter 30

Have An Affair

Okay, you've gotten married, you've had kids, and you've done all the things adults are supposed to do. And you're probably bored out of your fucking mind. You've memorized every one of your wife's favorite positions and are beginning to wonder if she's aware that there are others. Anyone looking at you would see a well-adjusted individual who's being a responsible family man. There's no time like the present to fuck that up. It's time to have an affair.

Cheating Vs. Affairs

Earlier in this book there was a chapter on unfaithfulness, and all of the things I said in that chapter apply to affairs, but there are other rules with affairs. The real advantage to having an affair is that you have just one person to worry about. If you're the sort that ends up fucking a nameless many, you're much more likely to be caught simply due to numbers. You're more likely to have more and better sex if you just stick to the one extra marital affair.

Remember, familiarity is sometimes a good thing when it comes to sex.

Develop A Code

With today's world of e-mails and text messages, it's a good idea to develop a code with your mistress. You're going to want to be able to say things without anyone who sees your communications knowing what the fuck you're talking about. Agree on a safe word that lets the other person know it's okay to talk freely and another word that means people might be watching or listening. If you even think of texting something like, "C U 2NITE", you're not ready to have an affair. Say something like, "CSI: Miami" to let her know you want to meet her at 9pm on Monday. The key here is to make all intimate communication easily explainable and invisible.

Don't Lie To Your Mistress...Much

The biggest problem with having an affair is that you've given someone the power to destroy your marriage. So the big message here is, 'Don't piss her off.' An angry mistress is worse than an angry wife because the mistress has nothing to lose. This is why it's best to lie as little as possible to your mistress. Except for the obvious stuff of course. Never tell her when you have sex with your wife. Never tell her when you're buying something for your wife. In fact never tell her when you've done anything at all nice for your wife that you could be doing for her instead.

The one thing you absolutely want to tell the truth about is the fact that you aren't leaving your wife. You should make this clear from the beginning. Promising your mistress you'll leave your wife is both stupid and insulting. They know better or at least should know better. And if they don't, when they realize it, they'll go nuts.

One more thing if you're actually dumb enough to think about leaving your wife for your mistress, please do everyone a favor and hit yourself in the head. The two things your mistress knows about you are that you're a liar and a cheat. And more importantly, that's also what you know about her.

It's Only Hot When It's Taboo

The sex you have in an affair will always be better than the sex you have with your spouse. You ever hear the phrase, "Stolen beer tastes better?" That's true. There's an added excitement when you know you might get caught. This is the same reason why messing around when you were a teenager was so much fun.

What you need to realize here is that you should never leave your wife for your mistress because if you do, then your mistress just becomes a girl you can have sex with rather than a girl you're not supposed to have sex with. And if you hook up with her, whether you believe it or not, sooner or later you're going to want another girl you're not supposed to have sex with.

The End of the Affair

Ending things can be difficult. It's best to end things before you're found out. So if it looks like people are catching on to what's going on, that's the time to end it. You want to be very clear on ending things that it's for the good of both of you. You can even say it helps solidify the relationship so that now you don't have to worry about being found out anymore. Don't dump your mistress. Talk about it and come to a mutual decision on the how things are going to end. Are you going to remain in each other's lives or disappear? Are you going to still meet up for the occasional quickie? Decide these things now. Don't leave them up to chance.

If your mistress is the sort who won't agree to end things and you need to end them for some reason, then this is what you have to do. Get rid of all evidence that you two ever had an affair. Steal any gifts back that can be traced to you. Erase any emails. Do everything possible to erase yourself as an intimate figure in her life. And if she tries to out your relationship, call her crazy. I know it's harsh but so is divorce. This of course won't work if you haven't covered your tracks effectively so cover your tracks. And if all else fails, turn to the next page.

Chapter 31

Get Divorced

They say that no man is an island and that's true. I think we're actually more like countries than islands. And if we are countries, then the contract of marriage is a lot like two allies signing a treaty. You're in a sense saying, "You are our most favored nation." Generally this is a mutually beneficial pact that betters both nations.

However, if marriage is a treaty, then divorce is a declaration of war. And as anyone who knows anything about war will tell you, it's not always the most powerful side who wins, it's the side with the better strategy.

A Build Up of Forces

Nobody wants war, but there are times when it's inevitable. When the shit hits the fan in your marriage, you'd better be ready. And there's nothing better to help in the war effort than powerful allies. Before you've moved out, before she's taken half your stuff, before she's stabbed you with a nail file, you should find out who your friends are and who her friends are. You can do this in the preliminary stages. All you have to do is call them up for advice after an argument and see what they say. If they seem to take your side no matter what you did wrong, these are your boys. Remember them, you'll need them later.

If you even think that things might be heading towards divorce, you should contact a divorce lawyer. This guy will tell you where you really stand and what your situation really is. This is a vital piece of information. You may want to fake a reconciliation just to get the relationship to a point where you're in a better position for a divorce. But you won't know you need to do that without getting a lay of the land and that's what lawyers are for. Most divorce lawyers will give you a free half hour consult. You should talk to at least three and then make your plan.

Try not to get emotional about it. Remember that in divorce it's just a matter of losing as little as possible more than it is winning.

An Act Of War

In every divorce there is the one act that severs ties and ends any chance of reconciliation.

Whether it's an affair, an argument, or an awkward situation with somebody's sister, once it has happened things are no longer the same. No matter how nice your spouse used to be, no matter how close you once were, you must understand that after that act has occurred, they are the enemy until the divorce is done and perhaps for the rest of your life.

Rules of Engagement

One of the first rules of combat is that you do not trust your enemy. This means that once things are over you must assume every word your spouse says is a lie. Do not believe a word of it. More importantly do not allow yourself to get angry about it or about what others might be saying about you. Remember, you know who you are and what you've done and you're okay with that. If you weren't you would have killed yourself a long time ago.

Deception goes both ways. Give your spouse as little information as possible. If you can lie without being caught, lie. If you can avoid contact with them, do so. Let your up-until-recently-significant-other attempt to spread rumors or lies or whatever else. The calmer you behave, the better you look.

Another thing to keep in mind is that you should avoid any sort of drugs for the duration of this. A beer every now and then is fine, but the last thing you want is a drug charge or an accusation that you're an alcoholic. The judge doesn't know you and is only going to get what you two give him to decide what happens. Don't give anyone any leverage against you.

You're also going to want to avoid the appearance of any other relationship. This doesn't mean you can't have a lover at a time like this. Admittedly having someone new is a great way to get over the divorce, but do what you can to hide it. You're trying not to look like the bad guy here. If you bring your new 19-year-old girlfriend to court it's not going to look good.

Exit Strategy

Once all is said and done, you'll either have what you want or not. Whatever the case, the war is over and you're still around. Enjoy that fact. Your ex may have tried to destroy you, but you're still standing.

Now is the time to have a drink or three. Now is also the time to say anything you like about your ex to anyone you want. Feel free to be an asshole. And at all times refer to your ex as just that. Do not call her by name. She will now and forever be known as 'the ex'.

No matter how bad things get, no matter what happens, just remember that people often mention how getting married was a mistake but they never say that about getting divorced.

Chapter 32

Go On A Bender

Whether you know it or not, this is the chapter you've been waiting for. Maybe you looked at the table of contents and just flipped to this chapter. Maybe you've been reading as quickly as possible to get here. Maybe you're just surprised the chapter didn't show up sooner.

The fact of the matter is that going on a proper binge requires both skills and planning. Many people will tell you that the whole idea of a bender is to NOT plan, but they miss the point. We are not trying to crash the jet of our life into the ground as fast as possible. We are trying to rocket that jet straight towards the ground and manage to pull up at the last possible second. It's a miraculous feat and not something you can just randomly attempt. Doing this wrong can result in not just the ruination of your life but no chances of ever being able to do it again and let's face it, the fun of plummeting is the fall, not hitting the ground.

First off, you need to determine what sort of duration you want your bender to be. I recommend between one and six months. Decide in advance how long you plan to live this way and tell no one. You need this to be a solo event. What we're going for here is the sort of bad craziness that will mark you by friends and family as a person on their way down. What they won't know is you'll have the time of your life doing it.

Lose Your Friends

I don't mean do things to piss off your friends until they leave you. Rather I mean stop hanging out with them entirely. Don't return phone calls. Don't go to their parties. Avoid anyone you care about as much as possible during the entire duration of your bender. And do not explain to these people what your intentions are. If they ask why you seem so distant, just say, "I need some space right now." The reason for this is simple; eventually you're going to want to return to your old life and what you're about to get involved in is the sort of thing you won't want friends and family really knowing a whole lot about. Cutting them out temporarily is for their own good.

Gain New Friends

Now that you've gotten rid of anyone who will disapprove of what you're doing, it's time to get some enablers. These people we will call 'new friends'. You will find these people at bars and in drug houses. You'll find them at parties where there is only bad beer and more than fifty people. These are people who are on their own self-destruction kick and will help you along your way. You will know these people by the fact that you'd never introduce them to your parents. The other telltale fact is that these friends are the sort of people you know you don't want to know the rest of your life. To do this right, you want these people to care about you more than you care about them.

How do you make people who don't care about themselves care about you? It's easy. All you need is to provide something that they want that they have difficulty getting on their own. Find a decent pot connection. Learn the art of needle sticking. (Junkies value someone who can find a quick vein). Lose your nice apartment and get a shitty dive they can all hang out at. If you have extra money, be generous with it. As soon as you can offer them something they value, you'll be on their friends list.

One other thing about these new friends; do not tell them anything about your real life unless you have to. You do not want these people looking you up months after you're done with your bender. Ideally you don't want these people to even know your last name.

Do Drugs

Now when I say 'do drugs', I'm going to suggest you begin with alcohol. During a bender alcohol should be consumed several times a day. You'll also probably want to get into the other drugs that I covered at the beginning of this section. Feel free to get a little out of hand here, but not too much. Don't stick with any one drug for too long. Avoid actually becoming addicted to anything. The key to a good binge is being able to pull out of it at the end.

During your binge you should spend as little time as possible sober. During a proper bender you may find yourself in bed with unattractive people, eating bad food, going to awful places, doing criminal things, and perhaps getting arrested, and/or beaten. All of these things are much more tolerable and occasionally even enjoyable if you're under the influence of a few drugs. And not being on said drugs can be outright dangerous. You do not want to be the only sober guy in a drug house.

Have Random Sex

As far as anyone knows you're crashing and burning. You've got nothing to live for and nothing to lose. You're drunk and crazed. The last thing in the world you should have is standards. Your taste in members of the opposite sex (or the same sex for that matter if you're into that) should consist of one quality: that they want to have sex with you. This will expose you to a wide variety of people you wouldn't otherwise see naked. You'll probably want to be remotely safe about this but that shouldn't be a priority. After all, too much focus on safety and you lose the point of the binge.

You must keep in mind that these are not soulmates. These are not girlfriends, boyfriends, significant others, or even lovers. They are at best fuck buddies and most likely not even that. They are people you've fucked. One other note, there's no reason to let them know that's how you feel.

Appear to Hit Bottom

Towards the end of your bender you should plan the final chapter. Have a big party. Tell them all it's your birthday or something. Have it at a place you don't care about and will never return to. Do not have it at a place that has your name on it. Encourage absolutely everyone you don't respect to attend. Tell them all to bring all the drugs they can find or steal.

Now here's the key to this. You need to start drinking about three hours before the party starts. You want to be drunk off your ass when things finally get going. And when the party starts going you want to continue to drink. You can't fake this. You absolutely must be as drunk as possible without passing out.

Next, at somewhere between one and three in the morning you need to get mad at something or someone. And then you need to leave mad. This shouldn't be too hard. Alcohol tends to make getting pissed off a lot easier. Yell at the top of your lungs. Be sure to make a big scene. And then you leave. Don't drive. Walk off into the early morning with vengeance on your mind. Bring a full bottle of whisky you've been saving for this occasion. Drink it until you pass out somewhere.

Return to Your Life

This is a bit tricky. What you need to do here is find that one person in your life who was the last to give up on you. The one who kept calling after you started your binge. You need to call your best friend. You should do this from a pay phone or at the very least a phone that isn't yours. Ideally you'll do this the night after you 'hit bottom'. You tell your best friend that these past few months were all a mistake and that you're sorry. Tell him how you want to make things right again and live how you used to.

If possible you should stay with this friend until you're well again. You're going to need someone who disapproves of your recent lifestyle in order to get out of it. Get rid of any and all contact information you had with the 'new friends' and make sure any contact information they have is out of date. Don't worry. Those kind of people don't go looking for anyone for very long.

Returning from a bender isn't easy and it isn't fun, but it's the price you pay for surviving. One last thing you should know. You should go on no more than three full-blown benders in your lifetime. Preferably these should be after major events (the death of a friend or relative, a big break up, turning 30, it's Thursday). It helps the people in your life forgive you if they think there's an explanation for your descent into debauchery. Also keep in mind that on consecutive benders you need 'new friends' for each one because 'new friends' should never be old friends. The past as always, should be left in the past. And if you don't think you've quite recovered from the last bender, well that's what Part Three is for.

Part 3

Recovery

Recovery means different things for different people. Most of the things in this book are things that are fairly easy to either integrate into your life or leave behind. But sometimes ruining your life can take turns that no book could possibly predict.

It's times like these that you may need to take some drastic measures. Recovery isn't so much reforming as it is finding ways to survive in order to continue your journey. Ruining your life is an ongoing process. It's a way of life. It's not a destination. The secret to ruining your life is realizing that there is no point where it's ruined. Ruining your life is just like enjoying your life. The difference is you're not so obsessed with doing the right thing or doing the healthy thing. Instead you're obsessed with doing the wrong thing right.

I've put this section in here for the times when things have gotten out of hand. This is for the times when you need a break from the craziness or maybe just a different kind of craziness.

The ideas in this next section are markedly different from the rest of the book. That's intentional. These are your contingency plans. It's what to do when all else fails. It's how you recover from the bender that won't end.

And remember once you've recovered, there's no reason in the world not to begin the descent again.

Chapter 33

Disappear

If you want to ruin your life properly, you need to learn how to disappear. People hate it when you do this. You are supposed to be home when they call. You are supposed to go to work. You are supposed to go home. You are supposed to remain in one region and not leave without saying where you are going. In this age of cellphones, Facebook, and email, you are supposed to be able to be found. Well in short, screw that.

There are times I don't answer my cellphone. I don't listen to my voicemails. I don't even have a landline. I don't want to be found all the time and really whether you know it or not, neither do you.

You see the problem with being able to be contacted at any time is that this may make people think you are reliable and this leads to responsibilities. Responsibilities are not good. Not when you're ruining your life. And in most circumstances responsibilities are just things people want you to do because they don't want to do it.

Why You Should Disappear

Let me explain my Paisley Shirt Theory. I think that life is like a Paisley Shirt: the closer you are to it, the less you can see what it is. Distance is needed to truly understand what is going on. Without distance, you will just keep looking at the pattern without ever seeing that it's just a shirt. You must get out of your life to see it. Perspective is a wonderful thing.

After all, how will you know how far down the spiral you are if you don't take a look once in a while?

It is said that most people are born, live, and die within a 25-mile radius. Coincidentally this is the same radius as many nuclear weapons. Why would you want to regulate yourself to being part of that statistic? You're not some cold war relic. You're a person with feet and the ability to drive a car, even if it is stolen. Go somewhere. See the world. Get out of your area code. Wouldn't it be nice if not all of your stories took place in the same state or even the same country?

Travel is one of the best ways to get to know yourself. Change your surroundings and all that's left the same is you. This is important. You need to know who you are in order to properly ruin your life.

Another thing to keep in mind is that if you start disappearing from time to time, then people will get used to it. This means that when you go on a three-day John-Belushi-would-have-been-proud binge inside your own apartment people will probably not worry. They'll just think you've gone 'walkabout' as our Australian friends would say. My mother used this little strategy to have an affair for twenty years. Personally, I think there are better uses for it. But I'll leave that to you. Use your imagination.

How To Disappear

Modern technology has made it increasingly difficult to successfully disappear, but it can still be done. The first thing you want to do is leave your cellphone at home. Also bring cash. Checks and credit cards can be traced. Do NOT leave a note. You're doing this for you. If people don't understand, good. That makes you mysterious.

Let's be clear here. You do not want people to think you are predictable and reliable. If you leave a note, if you leave the number where you'll be, if you think of telling one person where you're going, you do not know how to disappear. Telling people where they are is how fugitives get caught. If you tell anyone where you are, people will find you and your life will catch up with you. Your break will be interrupted in the worst possible way. Author Michael Crichton writes in his autobiography that he was informed of his father's death while on vacation with his beautiful girlfriend. This made him cut the vacation short and ruined the whole trip. This happened because someone knew where he had gone. Learn from his mistake. If people can find or contact you, you have not successfully disappeared.

Pick a destination. Preferably some place you haven't been before that is remote but inexpensive. Rent a small room in a motel by the beach or something. Buy a hat. Wear clothes you don't normally wear. If you see someone you know, pretend to be someone else. This is a vacation from your life. It is the thing almost everyone needs and almost no one ever does.

What you're doing is taking time for yourself. Sometimes even in the course of ruining our lives, we get so busy that we don't take time. Not time to just smell the roses, but to watch the roses grow while you drink a martini and think of what you're going to do next for your life. You should do this at least once a year, but it's preferable to do it once a season. Or if possible, once a month. Hell, you should disappear every Wednesday through Saturday.

Ruining your life can take a lot out of you. This is your chance to regroup and plan. This is also your time to do anything you don't normally do. Always wanted to try gambling? Parasailing? What about a prostitute or two? What about gambling and spending the winnings on parasailing with prostitutes? The more outrageous the idea, the better. The reason for this is that if someone asks where you were, the best thing to say is the truth. Just make sure the truth is not believable.

"Where'd ya go last weekend, Bill? I tried to call you."

"Oh, I was eating sushi off the breasts of a 19-year-old on the coast."

"Yeah, right."

The best way to get away with anything is to make it unbelievable and the best way to ruin your life is to have an unbelievable life. Look at Jimmy Buffett or Hunter S. Thompson.

Stay Gone

How long should you disappear? Well, that's entirely up to you. It should at least be three days otherwise it's just a weekend trip. But maybe you'll find that this new life suits you. Maybe after getting a good look at your old life, you'll think you should stay away from it. Well, nothing is stopping you. There's no reason in the world that you shouldn't disappear and never come back…unless of course, you happen to like your old life. If that's the case, go back home. Just keep in mind the beach is always there and people disappear every day.

Chapter 34

Go To Church

I suppose the last thing you'd expect to find in a book that endorses lying, cheating, drinking, and dating teenagers is something about religion. But let's face it, if ever a guy managed to ruin his life, it was good old J.C. I mean he had everything going for him: good family connections (you can't get better than God as your dad), ability to walk on water, heal the sick, cure the blind, and best of all, he can turn a pitcher of water into a pitcher of wine. Now THAT'S a party trick. But then what happened? The dude got crucified. Now that's a level of ruining your life that not even I will endorse.

Don't worry. I'm not going to tell you how Jesus was the son of God and how you'll be saved from Hell if you believe in him, because for all I know it could be bullshit. To me, personal beliefs are just that. I'm not going to tell you what to believe.

Jesus Saves....You Money

Almost all churches despite their different denominations are the same: Greeting, song, prayer, song, offering, sermon, song. Not exactly my idea of fun. Especially considering the fact that most church songs are as full of God as they are bereft of talent. So why, oh why, should you go to church? Simple: Resources. Never mind the fact that hymns are boring and sermons almost always sound the same. (That can't really be helped when your source material is 2000 years old.) Never mind that a lot of the people there are just old people afraid of death. You're here for one reason and one reason only: The church has more pull than you do.

The first church I ever belonged to was a Quaker church. (And no, that doesn't mean like Amish people or the guy on the oatmeal box.) Within a month of joining that church I was going to Mexico for a fraction of what it would have cost me to go alone. Sure, it was a "Mission Trip" where we were painting a church and putting up a fence, but it was still Mexico. And I was sixteen. What other possible way would I get to go to Mexico with my girlfriend and not have my parents along?

Over the next couple years, I went to Portland, Hayden Lake, Mt. Rainier, and a bunch of other places rarely paying a dime. Churches are by and large volunteer organizations and the more you volunteer, the more you get to do.

Once you get yourself established in a church, you can even suggest events to attend or create. It's like having your own travel agency. Do it the right way and you get to call the shots without taking your wallet out of your pocket.

God's Neat, Let's Eat

Just about any church function, even if it doesn't involve travel, involves food. There is always free coffee, and usually there are cookies and whatever else. And of course there are the potlucks. You should offer to volunteer as much as possible. The more you do this, the more clout you get in the church and the more people tend to like you.

If you're anything like me, you like food. And the best kind of food is free food. Sure, there won't be any beer, but you can buy beer with the money you saved by eating at church.

Christians Are Easy

It has been said many times that when it comes to sex, Christians are easy and for the most part, they are. Being into God doesn't necessarily mean not being into sex. Sure, there are those who actually want to 'save' themselves for marriage, but even in church, they are the minority. A good amount of people in church on Sunday have had one hell of a Saturday night. After all no matter what they do, they can always be forgiven.

There's just something about growing up in a restrained belief system that makes a lot of Christians like sexual slingshots, the greater the resistance, the further you can get with them.

Forgive Me

The real allure to Jesus, if you ask me, is the ability to repent and the propensity for Christians to forgive. Hanging out with true Christians can be really wonderful because no matter how badly you fuck up, they will forgive you as long as you seem to genuinely feel bad for whatever it is you did. This is why people in prison 'find Jesus'. Sure the courts won't let them off the hook, but Jesus will. Besides what's life in prison compared to afterlife in Heaven?

The other thing about Jesus is that it's a safe bet. If there's no God, you'll be just as dead believing in Jesus as not. But if there IS a God and he happens to ask, "Do you believe in Jesus?", it'd be nice to be able to say, "Yes. You bet your ass I do.", don't you think? I mean you've got nothing to lose there.

So just to recap, finding Jesus = free travel, free food, easy sex, and possible eternal salvation. Not bad, eh? However, if you ask me the best part of going to church is what they like to call 'the fellowship'. See, church friends are more likely to help you than any other friends you have. This is the power of belonging to a group. And if you ever get into some legal trouble, it helps to be able to say that you're an active member of a local church.

And as for how this ruins your life, well, how's attending church every Sunday morning and singing hymns like "When I Wasn't Worthy" next to a tone-deaf 98-year-old sound for ruining your life? I thought so.

Chapter 35

Go To Therapy

Let's face it. If you've actually tried the things in this book, you are one fucked up bunny. You need help. And not the sort of help you're going to get from any book. You need therapy, man.

Now I know what you're thinking. Why on earth would you want to go talk to someone who doesn't even know you and tell her all of your problems and pay her rather than just going to the local bar and telling your problems to someone who'll at least pour you a drink for your money? I'll tell you why, because therapy is the ultimate alibi.

An Outside Opinion

Ask any therapist if they are going to help you and they'll say something like, "I'll help you help yourself." Believe it or not this isn't far from the truth. The single best thing about going to therapy is that you can finally talk to someone who isn't part of your life. You don't have to worry about telling them something and having the wrong people find out about it. This is a person you can tell secrets to.

I should also point out that when I say 'secrets', I mean affairs, lies, and that sort of thing. Do NOT tell her any crimes you have done, are doing, or plan on doing. There are laws about things like that. Keep it real, but keep it non-criminal.

Still, the single best thing about going to a therapist is getting an informed opinion from someone outside of your life who can't possibly have any ulterior motives. This alone is worth the money they charge.

Honesty

The other nice thing about having a therapist is that she is the one person in your life you can tell the truth to. In fact you can even tell her about the lies you've told other people. Contrary to what you might think, a good therapist will not condemn you for your behavior whatever it is.

Of course given you can't tell her about crimes and there's a chance you may be committing some crimes, you might wonder how you can tell the truth and not talk about these things. The answer is easy. Just talk about the feelings. Talk about how you feel about something that happened. The therapist will just assume you aren't ready to talk about specifics.

Breakthrough

You will not be healed by this experience. Odds are you will not uncover some past event that explains everything about you. What will happen is you'll get a better understanding of yourself and where you are in your life. This is vitally important on the long spiral down. You need to know how far away the ground is. Ruining your life takes a lot of hard work. Going to therapy is a good way to see how well that work is paying off. While talking to your therapist you'll probably notice that she's interested in the stories you have to tell. It's not just because she's trying to do her job. It's because you're living the life she secretly wants to live. You are not working 40 hours a week, taking two weeks of vacation a year, and watching the news every night. You are not part of the machine. You're a loose nut that's flown off the machine and no one knows where you're going to land.

Unless you find some special connection with your therapist you should only go for about six months. This is enough time to get a feel for what therapy is about and it's more than enough time to figure out where you're going. The other part of this is that you probably have better things to spend your money on. Therapy is like taking your car for a tune up; it's important to do from time to time but if you find your car is always in the shop something is wrong with the mechanic. This is why it's good to try other therapists every couple years or so.

Therapy isn't for everybody. If you're clearly psychotic and an obvious danger to your fellow man you should stay away from people who can have you put away. Also stay away from me. I have enough psychopaths in my life.

Chapter 36

Go To Las Vegas

This is it. The last chapter of Ruin Your Life. Why is this the last chapter? Because everything you have learned so far can be best used in Las Vegas. Don't believe the movies or the commercials or anything else. The one thing this city was built to do is ruin your life. This is the end of the line. When you've finally exhausted your resources, your family, and your friends it's time to go to Las Vegas.

Vegas Baby! Uh…No

First off before you even head off into the desert, you need to stop thinking of it as 'Vegas'. Vegas is where all the fucking tourists go. You may be from out of town, sure, but you are not a fucking tourist.

The purpose of this trip is simple: to burn out rather than fade away. This is a place where drinks are free, public drunkenness is encouraged, and getting laid is easier than clapping your hands. Prepare for the ride of your life

People come here to misbehave. They expect to lose money, to do things they'll regret, and act like complete idiots. In other words, everybody there is trying to ruin his or her life…for a weekend. These people are amateurs! You however, have become the professional. You know how to lie, how to drink, how to throw a party, and how to fight. You're ready for anything and the last thing you are is a sucker. For that reason alone you're not a tourist.

It's The Journey, Not The Destination

The quick and easy way to Las Vegas is to find an airline special and fly your ass out there. This is also the least interesting and most pain in the ass way to do it. Airplanes are for leaving, not arriving.

Instead, what you should do is tell all your friends you're going to Las Vegas and see who wants to chip in gas money and come with you. It's time to put you and your car to the ultimate road test. After a high-speed drive across the Nevada desert to the City of Sin, you know your car and yourself better than ever before. There's something about driving through hundreds of miles of nothing that is deeply satisfying, especially when you see the Las Vegas skyline in the distance. It is the Promised Land for all you non-believers.

On your way to Las Vegas you should stop in the desert at night and look up. All those little white things up there are stars. You've probably never seen so many and even if you have it's still a good idea to take a minute and look up. It's a good reminder of how insignificant you really are. Remember, there are more galaxies out there than there are people on Earth.

You are just a flea on the dog of the world.

Free Ride

I'm not going to talk about gambling much. The thing about Las Vegas is that all the gambling tends to make everything else cheaper. There's nowhere else you can get a real steak dinner for $3.99 and you don't even have to gamble to get that.

Want something to drink with that steak? Go to any bar with video poker machines. Put twenty dollars in, the bartender will ask you what you want to drink and give it to you free of charge. The thing about video poker is that it's not a timed game. You can play as slowly as you like and most places will just keep the drinks coming and if they don't, cash out your twenty bucks and go to any of the thousand other casinos within walking distance.

Need a place to stay? No, you don't. All you need is a place to crash. This is easy. Go to any of the big hotel casinos and look for the loudest group of people you can find. Odds are that before the night is over they'll all be drinking in some hotel suite. Follow them to the party and pass out. They'll wake you up in a few hours and you're ready to go. If you want a place to stash your stuff, go find and rent a locker for a buck or two. The nice part about being from out of town is that you can do whatever you want and you don't have to worry about making a bad impression. It's not like these people will ever see you again.

Viva Las Vegas

If you find yourself actually getting into legal trouble at all in Las Vegas, you should leave as quickly as possible. There aren't a lot of laws in Nevada, but the laws they have are significant and the prison sentences are long.

Then again, maybe you'll find you don't want to leave Las Vegas. You won't be alone in that thought. Las Vegas is one of the largest growing cities in the world and it's in the middle of the desert. That should tell you something.

They say that what happens in Vegas stays in Vegas, but really there's no reason you shouldn't too. Enjoy.

Author's Note

The idea behind this book was not to let people learn from my mistakes. I wanted them to learn to make my mistakes correctly. It's about doing bad things well. More often than not if you ask someone how to lie, have an affair, or go out with teenagers, the only advice you'll get is, "Don't." What has been needed is a guidebook for the Fallen. If I've done my job right, this is just such a guidebook.

And like any good guidebook, I acknowledge that it isn't complete. There are things I haven't even mentioned in this book. There are some things that really do need to be experienced to be understood. Others are things I feel other books have covered well enough that I don't need to. And still others are things I've simply never dared try.

In many ways, this is an autobiography. Everything mentioned in this book comes from my own personal experience. Most of these things happened due to my philosophy that I'd rather regret doing something than not doing it. The consequences of these actions have been many and in some cases, severe. I have been ruining my life for many years and I've actually gotten quite good at it.

There are people who I've watched try to do the same things I've done. Frequently they'd miss the point or make a critical error that would result in catastrophe. The purpose of this book is to send you down a dark path but to make sure you stay on that path.

Like I said in the beginning of this thing, if you actually try anything in this book, you're on your own. I've specifically and repeatedly told you that doing these things will likely ruin your life. If I haven't been clear enough yet, read this next sentence: DO NOT TRY ANYTHING IN THIS BOOK. There. Now you're truly on your own.

I don't expect I'll make much money with this book. That's not the point though. The idea was simply to get it out there. I remember thinking when I was younger how older people were always saying "If I knew then what I know now." I always thought those fuckers were selfish bastards. They had knowledge I wanted and they didn't share it. I said back then that once I knew, I'd write about it. And now I have. You're welcome.

- Jack Cameron
  October 2007

Ruin Your Life Revisited

It's been seven years since I first published Ruin Your Life. Since then I've sold over a thousand copies in softcover and as a Kindle book. There are copies of this book in Afghanistan and in prison. I've had people I don't know tell me it's their favorite book and I've had my own father tell me to get it out of his house.

This new edition was created thanks to both popular demand and the good people at Dark Repast who wanted it as part of their catalog. When they asked me to put together a new edition of this, I thought about it for a while and decided that even seven years later, there isn't much to add. Ruin Your Life is the book I wanted it to be. In this edition I've made a few minor edits and changed the formatting a bit but the core of the book remains the same. This is a book to help people do the wrong things right.

Many people have asked if I'm coming out with a sequel to Ruin Your Life, but I'll be honest. I simply don't think I have it in me. I've joked that this is a books about 'all the mistakes I made in my 20s'. I'm in my late 30s now. I'm done with Ruin Your Life but I have many more books to write.

Thanks for reading.

- Jack Cameron
  February 2014

Special Thanks

A project like this could not have possibly been completed without the help of some friends. (In somewhat random order):

Mimi Levenson
Nate & Kristen Kirby
Jim Clawson
Mark Daniels
Geoff Gibbs
Phil & Jenny Woodard
Robert Hazelton
Sam Cameron
Jenya Campbell
Bridget Howe
Matt Dolge
David Sullivan
Edward Gibbs V
Gabe & Jaime Vogt

About The Author

Jack Cameron is a writer and a consultant. He has written and published books, screenplays, instruction manuals, knowledge bases, and websites. He's consulted on numerous Kickstarter campaigns that have crowd funded over $500,000.

Currently he maintains a website dedicated to his hometown of Tacoma and a personal website. You can find him online at:

Twitter: @jackcameron
JackCameron.com
TacomaStories.com

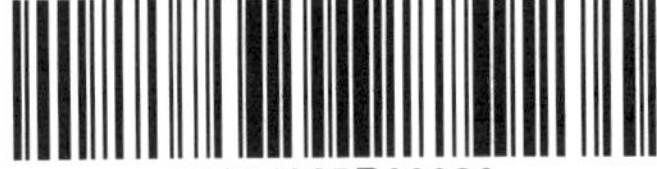
28074065R00080

Made in the USA
Charleston, SC
31 March 2014